rachel weeping

BRETT MICHAEL INNES

TRACEY McDONALD PUBLISHERS

First published by Tracey McDonald Publishers, 2015
Office: 5 Quelea Street, Fourways, Johannesburg, South Africa, 2191
www.traceymcdonaldpublishers.com

ISBN 978-0-620-63481-6
e-ISBN (ePUB) 978-0-620-63482-3
e-ISBN (PDF) 978-0-620-63483-0

Text design and typesetting by Reneé Naude
Cover photography and design by Brett Michael Innes
Back cover photograph of Brett Michael Innes © Huw Morris
Edited by Alison Lowry
With contributions from Anel Alexander, Corine Du Toit and Sandra Vaughn
Printed and bound by Interpak Books (Pty) Ltd

jeremiah 31:15

'A voice is heard in Ramah,
lamentation, weeping, great mourning,
Rachel weeping for her children and
refusing to be comforted,
because they are no more.'

prologue

THIS COULD BE the last time I'm here.

The thought was sobering and Rachel forced herself to be still, to try and take in the colours, smells and textures of the beach that stretched beyond her in both directions. She looked out at the aquamarine waters and watched as the fishermen used their lantern sails to harness the wind to pull their dhows back to shore after what looked like an unsuccessful day's fishing. The light of the midday sun was softer than usual, but it still bounced off the white beach sand and illuminated the whole area in a dazzling glare that made everything look brand new.

Save for a few beach dogs and children, the place was more or less empty, with the residents of the village either escaping the tropical heat inside their grass huts or waiting for the fish to bite. A few seagulls hovered above the water and further along the beach she saw an elderly woman collecting coconuts that had fallen during the night.

Rachel had walked this beach many times in her twenty-eight years on this earth. She knew its character and had witnessed its changes. What had once been a tiny fishing village guarded by the Bazaruto Archipelago had slowly grown into the holiday destination of Inhassoro, bringing with it tourists and money. This had all changed in 2000 when Cyclone Leon-Eline had slammed into the coast near Beira, bringing with it a season of floods, starvation and poverty, and making international headlines when a local woman, Sofia Pedro, was forced to give birth in a tree while the floodwaters rushed and churned below her. That had been ten years ago, when Rachel was eighteen, and the years that followed were difficult for the local community. While the holiday resorts eventually found ways of climbing back onto their feet, the villagers were still struggling.

Closing her eyes, Rachel listened to the sounds of the beach so familiar to her, the deep pounding of the waves as they broke, then their gentle lapping against the shore as they moved to a rhythm that came from deep within the heart of the ocean. As the song of the waves faded into the background, she heard the sharp cries of the seagulls and the voices of the fishermen as they called out to each other, pieces of their conversations about life and the catch travelling across the water to her ears.

Her father had been one of those fishermen until he had injured his leg; now he found work by repairing the same nets he'd once spent his early mornings casting out over the dark waters of the Indian Ocean. The cyclone had left the seas empty and what had once been the backbone of the village was now crippling its development. The fishermen would spend their days out at sea only to return with empty nets and the poison of hope that promised them tomorrow would be better.

Rachel breathed in deeply. The crisp salty fragrance of the sea and the tang of the morning's catch mingled with the aroma of baking pão that drifted in from the village. When she was twelve she had sat with her mother and the other women in the market who sold the delicious fresh bread rolls. Her mother would always let her eat the first pão of the day and she would take pleasure in tearing the warm, doughy bread apart and watching the steam rise through the air. These days it was only the wealthy who could afford the pão and there would be no free bread given to children who spent their mornings working in the market.

The smell of the pão instinctively made her lick her lips but it was only the salty ocean air she could taste, humid and tangible on her skin. She placed the last segment of the mandarin she'd been eating into her mouth and felt the tart explosion of its sweet juice as she bit into it. What had once been a common meal was now a rare treat. Her mother had given her the fruit for her last breakfast in Inhassoro.

Her eyes still closed, Rachel focused on the warmth of the Mozambican sun and the contrast that the cool of the ocean wind brought as it blew over the drops of perspiration on her forehead. She dug her toes into the sand, breaking through the crust that had been dried out by the morning sun and into the damp layer below, feeling for the water left behind by the tide.

She put her hand on her belly, felt how the skin beneath her shirt was warm and the flesh firm. It would still be a few more weeks before she would start to show but she could already sense that things were different inside her body. She could feel that she wasn't alone in her skin, that there was someone separate and independent growing inside her. The knowledge scared and inspired her at the same time. It filled her thoughts and occupied her dreams.

She was leaving Inhassoro for this person, going somewhere else so that the soul that was renting her body would have a chance at life, or at least a better life than the one Rachel had been given. She was leaving her family, her home and her beach for this new life, and going to a place she'd never been before.

But it wasn't only for her unborn child that she was going. Her parents were old now and unable to support themselves any more. She had looked for work in Inhassoro but had found nothing of value. She had even taken the bus to Maputo a few times and spent weeks calling on every hospital or clinic she could find, only to be told that they were either fully staffed or that they paid the same wages she would earn working in the fish market back home.

Mozambique had nothing for her and she needed a solution before her child was born. No one would hire a pregnant woman and so she knew she would have to secure employment before her condition became obvious.

Rachel opened her eyes and looked down to see a cowry shell at her feet, the porcelain of its mottled brown exterior speckled with white beach sand. She had seen thousands of these shells in her life and had either thrown them back into the water or made jewellery out of them but, for some reason, this one caused her to look twice. Maybe it was the emotion that was coursing through her heart today or just a desire to hold onto something that was 'home', something that wouldn't change, and she bent and picked it up.

She dusted the grains of sand from its surface and examined it. It was smooth in her hand and warm in the sunlight, the size of a small plum. She turned the egg-shaped shell over. Its flat white underbelly revealed a slit-like opening punctuated by blunt teeth. She held it up to her mouth and blew into the opening, expelling the sand that had gathered there over years. What had once been a living thing beneath the waters in the ocean had found its way into her hand.

Rachel slipped the cowry shell into her pocket and looked out to sea one last time before she turned and walked up the beach to her parents' grass hut. Her bag was packed. All that was left to do was say her goodbyes and go to the bus station.

She was leaving Mozambique. She was going to Johannesburg.

chapter 1

'RACHEL, I KNOW this is a conversation we've all been avoiding, but it's one that we need to have.'

Rachel looked across the twelve-seater wooden table at Chris and Michelle Jordaan. The light from the designer ceiling lamp shone harshly on the polished surface that separated her from the couple. She watched as the steam from three mugs of tea wafted slowly through the air between them. The gas heater in the corner of the stylish room glowed red as it tried to warm up the space but it didn't seem to be making much headway. Once the season started turning the cold always managed to find its way inside this house. It wrapped itself around Rachel's exposed ankles.

'It's been four weeks now,' Chris said. His face was covered in a layer of dark stubble – more the result of neglect than fashion. 'We need to decide what the next step forward for all of us is going to be.'

Rachel waited for him to continue, watching as he struggled to find the words. Michelle sat quietly at his side, staring at the table so that she did not have to look at Rachel. Her blonde hair, usually so perfectly groomed, was tied up in a rough ponytail, the darker roots clearly visible beneath the golden halo. Chris's brown hair had grown lighter over the almost six years that Rachel had worked for them and at the corners of his eyes now she could see permanent creases left by the smile that he had once worn so regularly.

'Look, Rachel,' Chris said, finding his words again, 'we've loved having you work here but we do understand if you want to move on.'

Rachel remained silent. She was trying to hear what Chris was really saying to her. He was a good man, this much she knew, but right now he was attempting to solve a problem and his loyalty would be to Michelle, who had now started to pick at a crack in the table's woodwork. Rachel had learned that she and Michelle were the same age when she had helped set up her 30th birthday party a few years back but this similarity had only served to remind her of how different they were to each other.

'If that is the case,' Chris continued, 'we'll compensate you well beyond what the law requ – '

'I'll stay.'

The statement cut Chris off in mid-sentence and pulled Michelle's eyes up from the table.

'Are you sure?' Chris said. 'Would you not like some time to think about it?'

'I will stay.'

Rachel reinforced her decision in a quiet tone that left the Jordaans with little room to question it. She, too, was surprised by how controlled she had been. She saw Chris glance quickly at Michelle.

Clearly neither of them had been prepared for an immediate answer and definitely not for this one.

Chris took his wife's hand and Michelle returned her attention to the crack in the table.

'Well, if that's what you want to do,' he said, 'then we're going to have to ask that you start working again on Monday – tomorrow. As you can see, the house needs some cleaning.'

He was right, it did need cleaning. Rachel had noticed it the moment she walked in, aware that her absence had been felt by the Jordaans and the beautiful structure that they called home. The black and white tiles in the entrance hall were dirty, the kitchen sink was filled with dirty dishes and utensils and, if she were to walk to the bathroom, she was certain that she would find a laundry basket stuffed full with the clothes that had piled up over the last few weeks.

'It's fine. Monday will be fine.'

'Are you sure, Rachel?' Chris asked, frowning slightly.

Rachel looked across at Chris and nodded her head once more, trying to convince Chris that she was. If they believed her statement then maybe, over time, she would too. She maintained eye contact with him as he searched her gaze for something that would contradict the answer she had just given.

She gave him nothing.

Then he looked away and directed his conversation towards Michelle, trying to make it seem as though she had been a part of this next decision when he was making it as he spoke.

'Well, then we'll be giving you an increase, since it was time to do that anyway. We can look at fixing up your room as well, so let us know if there is anything you would like put in, maybe a new two-plate cooker ...'

He was making an obvious effort to quell his discomfort with things. Rachel could feel bile rising in her throat as she listened to him list the offerings they would present to her as atonement.

'Thank you,' Rachel said. She saw a sliver of a smile return to Chris's eyes; he must be relieved that they had come to some kind of resolution. Rachel stared at him, not wanting to smile back but not wanting to be spiteful towards him either. Like her, he was also a victim, and when it came to Chris she could not bring herself to be malicious.

'Is there anything that you'd like to know or to ask us?'

'Would you be able to give me this month's wages tomorrow?'

'That shouldn't be a problem.'

Rachel nodded in acknowledgement and the three of them continued to sit in silence, unsure of how to proceed now that all that had needed to be said was out of the way. Rachel looked down at the table she polished on Tuesdays and Fridays. After a couple of minutes she realised that the Jordaans were waiting for her to end the dialogue.

'If that is all, then I'd like to go back to my room,' she said.

'Yes. Well. That's it,' Chris said, adding in Afrikaans: '*Dankie*.'

Rachel nodded again, this time in response to the expression of thanks. She couldn't really understand much of Chris and Michelle's home language, save for the few greetings and words she had picked up from them and their friends over the years. She stood up, the wooden chair scraping on the slate tiles and, more out of habit than intention, reached across to gather the mugs to carry them to the washing up area. Michelle jumped up quickly and motioned for her to stop.

'I'll do that.'

Rachel stopped and lowered her mug back to its place on the table. Straightening her shirt, she gave Chris a last look and left the room. There was silence behind her.

Michelle watched Rachel leave the kitchen and disappear down the dark passage. She heard the tired slap-slap of her slippers fading away on the tiles as she walked to the front door. Her thoughts were spiralling out of control. She heard the door open and close, followed by the sharp clang of the metal security gate.

She was supposed to go. She was supposed to take the money and go.

Numbly she carried the mugs through the state of the art kitchen to the sink. What on earth had possessed Rachel to stay? She poured the lukewarm tea down the plughole, the brown liquid running like a muddy waterfall over the dirty dishes already in the sink. She turned around. Chris was still sitting motionless at the table. She reverted to Afrikaans now that Rachel had gone.

'How are we meant to live like this?'

'We can't fire her,' Chris replied.

'Why not? You can't tell me this is a solution?'

'Of course it isn't, Michelle. But there's no way we can fire her.'

Michelle glared at her husband, knowing he was right but frustrated by the outcome of the evening's conversation. She watched as he calculated, as he tried to solve the problem they were faced with. Returning from the void, Chris looked up at her and exhaled.

'We'll just have to find a way to make this work,' he told her. 'For some reason she thinks that staying with us is better than leaving so we'll all just have to get on with it.'

Speechless, Michelle turned back to the sink. How Chris could simplify the situation so quickly into something that they would just figure out as they went along completely baffled her. He was treating it as though it were an increase in their electricity bill or a new brand of washing powder they were going to have to get used to.

She looked down at the mess in front of her – plates, bowls and cups that had collected over the weeks when she had not been able to bring herself to clean up. It wasn't that domestic work was beneath her; she had worked as a waitress at a pizzeria in high school and had seen much worse in her time there. For some reason, though, every time she had tried to bring herself to do the washing up all of her energy evaporated, an effect that seemed to grow with every new item that was added to the pile.

A heavy heart had given birth to heavy hands.

As she turned her back on the clutter she saw that Chris was no longer at the table. She listened to the sounds of the house, the laughter of a studio audience telling her that he was in the TV room. She switched the kettle on and opened the cabinet in front of her, taking out the remaining two clean mugs. Kitsch things only Chris would buy and which she would only use if they were alone. The purple one read 'Drama Queen' and the yellow one 'The Man, The Legend'. She placed a teabag in each.

'More tea?' she called out, her voice travelling past the four guest rooms, her study, the guest bathroom and into the TV room. The house had been built in the seventies when ceilings were high and rooms were spacious, very different to the new buildings that were cropping up in the northern suburbs of Johannesburg these days.

This was the first property she and Chris had bought together, and to say that it had needed 'a little TLC', as had been advertised when it first came onto the market, had been an understatement. They had followed the age-old wisdom of buying the bad house on a good street, but with Chris being an architect by profession, this had been less of a challenge to him than an exciting project. On the day they were given the keys to 76 5th Avenue in Parkhurst, they began a year of renovations that Michelle would have preferred to forget.

The faded carpets had been ripped up and replaced with large granite tiles, the old farm-style windows had been replaced by insulated, double-glazed ones, walls had been painted white and the divider between the kitchen and the living room been broken down. Each of the rooms had been decorated by a top designer, under Michelle's tasteful guidance, and the blend of furniture and art, a palette of greys, creams and beiges, was amplified by the textures of wood and wool.

The kitchen had been the worst and they had ended up gutting the entire thing and building it up from scratch. They put in marble counter tops, a gas stove, built-in cupboards, a corner pantry, a breakfast nook, a double-door fridge, a washing machine, a tumble dryer, a dishwasher and, in the corner, an industry level espresso machine.

Life was too short for instant coffee.

Michelle waited by the kettle for Chris to answer but heard nothing but the sound of channel surfing filtering through from the TV room. She took a breath to call out again but decided against it. She returned one teabag to its container and put the 'Drama Queen' mug back in the cabinet. She listened to the sound of the water as it boiled, staring at the patterns in the marble counter top. She still wasn't happy with the shade of white they had ended up with but had chosen not to say anything on the day she walked into the kitchen and found them already installed. These counter tops had become a reminder that, in life as in home makeovers, when it came to the interiors if she wanted something to be done right, she could not leave it up to Chris. He had been in charge on the day the counters had been installed and, when she pointed out later that the tops were a different shade to the sample they had agreed on, he had smiled that smile he always smiled and said no one would be able to tell the difference.

And now he was doing it again. Making decisions for her and then telling her that it wouldn't be that bad. But this wasn't a marble counter top; this wasn't a shade of off-white that she could just look past and pretend wasn't there. What added to her discomfort was that, unlike the counter tops, this was not Chris's fault. She was the one to blame for the situation they were trapped in and, as much as she wanted to look past it and pretend that it had never happened, she knew that if Rachel continued to work for them, this was not going to happen.

Michelle heard clawing at the door and turned to see Hugo, their small rescue dog of unsure origins, asking to go out into the garden. Michelle bent down to scratch the dog on its head before opening the door for him. When he'd finished doing his business outside Hugo hopped back up the steps into the kitchen and ran to his designer Max & Molly basket at the end of the room, where he would now curl up for the evening. Michelle smiled as she turned the lights off in the kitchen and made her way to the other side of the house. Were it not for Chris's 'no dogs in the bedroom' policy, she would have made sure Hugo's basket was at the foot of their bed.

Chris sank back in the deep leather sofa and flicked without any purpose or goal through the channels on the 49″ HD TV he and Michelle had bought earlier that year. The talk show he'd been watching had ended ten minutes ago but he didn't want to go to bed just yet. Even though they had gone for the most expensive cable TV package on offer, he was still amazed at how, when he wanted to watch something, there never seemed to be anything on.

He checked the PVR to see what they had recorded and scrolled through the episodes and movies they had on file. There were a few 20-minute sitcoms he could watch, but Michelle hadn't watched them yet and he knew she would be upset if he watched them without her. The first rule of watching a series when you're part of a couple was that you didn't watch an episode without the other person being present. The second rule was that you watched what your wife enjoyed watching which, for Chris, ruled out anything that had a hint of science fiction or horror. With only so many hours in the day, it meant that when he actually had the time to watch TV, he ended up watching some mundane reality series.

He scrolled past the backlog of reality shows, looking for the season finale of the science fiction series he knew he'd recorded the previous month. When he scrolled down to the end of their collection he realised that Michelle must have deleted it to make room for another show, something she wanted to watch.

Chris shook his head and picked up his silver iPad Air. He flicked through his apps while CNN played in the background. Michelle had given him the tablet for Christmas and, after a day of finding his way around it, he was hooked. He could spend hours trying out the different apps, his favourites being the social media ones.

He opened his Facebook account and a smile stole over his

face as he noted the red icon indicating that he had twelve new notifications. There were the usual Candy Crush invitations, which he immediately deleted, and a couple of likes and comments on a photo he'd posted of a cappuccino he had had that morning at his favourite cafe, The Whippet. Scrolling through his timeline, he liked a photo of a friend's baby, congratulated a couple who had just gotten engaged, and wished his cousin happy birthday, a date that he would never have remembered were it not for the reminder in the corner of the window on the page.

As he moved back up to the top of the timeline he noticed the 'PEOPLE YOU MAY KNOW' section and paused on the profiles of the people with whom the Facebook algorithm was suggesting he should consider interacting. Chris had to admit that he loved the voyeuristic side of Facebook. He could spend ages going through the profiles of old friends, even strangers sometimes, seeing how they lived and imagining how he might interact with them if they ever met up in person.

The first was Nicholas Alexander, a high school water polo teammate he hadn't seen in years. Chris entered Nicholas's profile but except for his profile picture, the security settings wouldn't allow him to see anything else. He hit 'ADD' anyway and returned to the 'PEOPLE YOU MAY KNOW' page to see who else was there.

Anja Fouche was next, an attractive redhead who had recently joined his company as PA to one of the directors. He couldn't say he knew her as they'd only really seen each other in passing. Her work station was across the open plan area from his office. Chris opened her profile and saw that she had no active security settings, which meant that her photos and information were freely available for anyone to see. Her 'ABOUT' section said that she was

34, Christian, non-political, had studied at Wits University and was, surprisingly, single. Chris went through to her photo albums, first looking up instinctively to see if Michelle was at the door before he took a proper look. He smiled as he scrolled through photographs of Anja in settings ranging from parties to mountain tops, European landmarks to the finish lines of triathlons. In all of them she looked vibrant and natural, the projection of a woman who was enjoying her independence and life.

He looked at the 'ADD' icon and for a brief moment considered touching it, attracted to the idea of being welcomed into this woman's digital life. Looking at the clock icon at the top of the screen, he saw that it was 22:54, well past his usual bedtime, and he turned the tablet off, making a mental note to keep an eye out for Anja at work the next day. Nothing would ever come from it, of course, but now that he had seen her life in photographs, he was curious to hear what her voice sounded like.

The domestic quarters were simple and unobtrusive, a free-standing building situated at the far end of the Jordaans' property. To call it a cottage would be generous for it was more a single room with an adjoining bathroom than the quaint image a cottage might conjure up.

Rachel sat on her bed, an old red biscuit tin in her cold hands.

The bitter cold of the winters in Johannesburg had been something she hadn't expected when she had first arrived in South Africa. She had never really adjusted to them. The cold still got to her and it seemed to have started even earlier this year. It wasn't that the temperatures were that low in winter – by European standards they wouldn't even be considered an autumn day, Chris had told her once – just that the houses in South Africa were designed for summer and they were unable to retain heat. While the winter days were sunny, the nights brought with them an icy cold that no heater could keep at bay. Rachel had found that the only way to secure herself a good night's sleep in winter was to go to bed with a jacket on, and doubling up socks so that her feet were protected by layers.

She popped the lid off the biscuit tin and placed it on the pillow beside her. She lifted out some papers while various keys and coins clunked along the tin's metallic base. She took out a small object that was secured in a twist of tissue paper and opened it carefully. It was a diamond ring. She held it up to the lamp and saw how the scratched gem still sparkled in the light. She had found the ring on a beach outside Inhassoro, a moment of fate that had left her believing that good things could sometimes happen to someone like her. She had had the ring valued in Johannesburg when she first arrived here and discovered that it was a four-carat diamond and worth about R8 000. Instead of pawning it, she decided at the time that it was probably wiser to keep it, safely tucked away in her biscuit tin with her other valuables. She didn't want to be spending the money she might get for it on foolish things.

The pawnshop would be a last resort for a day when she had no other options.

Next Rachel pulled out a wad of meticais, Mozambican bank notes, that she always kept untouched on the odd chance that she might need to make an emergency trip back to Inhassoro and didn't have time to exchange money. She placed the money on the small pine table that stood a few feet away from her bed.

The place she had called home for the last six years was a humble space, furnished mostly by hand-me-downs from the Jordaans and the few items she had purchased at the occasional yard sale in the neighbourhood. The kitchen and living area were joined to the bedroom, and there was a simple, separate bathroom. As small as her quarters were, she was fully aware that they were not to be looked down on; they were a huge step up from the tin shacks and shanty houses some other domestic workers lived in.

The table was the focal point of the little room. It included two chairs and it was used for eating at, reading and ironing. Not more than an arm's length away was a very basic kitchenette with a two-plate cooker and a sink. The sleeping area contained a single bed, a bedside table squeezed in beside it and, opposite, a chest of drawers in which Rachel stored everything she owned in South Africa. Balanced precariously on top of the chest was a small black and white TV.

Rachel took her passport out of the tin and placed it next to the money on the table. The gold coat of arms glowed against the blue background in the light from the bare bulb that hung from the ceiling in the middle of the room.

She dug inside the biscuit tin once more and pulled out a worn photograph which she brought closer to her face. The photograph was quite old now. She remembered the day it had been taken outside her parents' house, with a disposable Kodak camera. She had asked Sergio, the neighbour's son, to take the photo so that the whole family could be in it and had instructed him to take three just in case one came out blurry.

With a weary smile Rachel examined each of the faces, a moment that had been captured in time before she had journeyed to South

Africa. She had tried to explain to her parents how to pose for a photo but they didn't quite get it. Eventually she just told them to look at Sergio and not look away until she said they could. Andrea, her younger brother, who was 22 at the time, stood next to her mother while Rachel stood with her hands on her stomach, the tiny bump just beginning to show. Her father, despite her instructions, was looking to the side.

Rachel lowered the photograph to her lap. Off in the distance a shrieking siren signalled an emergency somewhere and she shuddered, trying to shut her ears to the sound. For a moment she felt dizzy and nauseous.

Revolving red neon lights reflecting on wet tar, flashing and turning.

The day her world had changed.

In an attempt to distract herself she recalled the conversation that she had had earlier that day with her mother, before her meeting with the Jordaans. Sundays were when she called her parents, usually on her walk home from church, from the pay phone outside the corner store. The pay phone was cheaper than a cellphone, and when it came to international calls, clearer too. Over the last few months her mother had been the only one able to walk to the phone in Inhassoro, her father's injury proving too painful for the journey.

This morning was no different to the previous calls, the only adjustment being the fact that she had skipped the church service and walked straight to the pay phone to make the call. The phone had rung five times before Anisia, the phone operator and baracca manager, answered it in Portuguese. Rachel, who had grown up with Anisia, returned her greeting and waited for her to pass the phone to her mother.

'Your father is doing well. He still can't walk very far but he can stand.'

'That's good, Mama.'

'There's been no water for five days now.'

'How much do you have?'

'We should have enough for three days if we don't wash. We managed to fill the bathtub and all our buckets the last time it came on.'

'Did you get the money that I sent you?'

'Yes. Your cousin went down to Kosi Bay and bought us food from the South African stores because there is nothing here. We used up all you sent.'

'I'll try to send more when I get paid next week.'

'Bless you, daughter. Is Maia with you?'

Rachel took the phone away from her mouth.

'Rachel?'

She took a deep breath. 'No, Mama. Maia's not with me.'

Her mother paused before speaking again.

'You sound ill, my child.'

'I'm fine, Mama. I'm just tired.'

'You must rest, Rachel. All that air pollution in that city is making you sick ...'

Rachel put her hand over the receiver as tears began to run down her face, hot emotion that she could not allow her mother to participate in.

'I need to go now, Mama. There are people waiting for the phone.'

She hung up before her mother could respond and leaned against the telephone, where she began to cry, ignoring the looks of passersby as she spilt the tears she had forbidden herself to share with her parents. She would tell them when she returned to Mozambique but, for now, she needed to be strong and figure out what the next step forward was going to be.

This job was money. It was the roof over her head. It was what kept her parents alive and what allowed her to remain in South Africa legally. She knew how hard it was to find stable work, especially as a domestic worker when there were ten other women ready and willing to do your job for half the wages. She had seen the trucks at the border post taking illegals back to Mozambique and had heard the stories of the weeks spent in detention centres if you were caught in South Africa without a work visa.

As she packed her things neatly back into the red biscuit tin fresh tears began to roll down her face, the quiet room offering no comfort to the pain she was feeling.

She had no choice.

chapter 2

RACHEL PULLED MAIA'S body closer to her belly, drawing comfort from the little girl as she preempted the shrill cry of the alarm clock that would signal the start of her day. They shared the single bed, an arrangement that worked well in the cold of winter but, with the summer being as hot as it had been this year, she found their proximity uncomfortable. She could feel Maia's chest rise and fall with each breath, her faint heartbeat drumming in time with her breathing.

The plastic clock radio on the bedside table clicked on and the room was filled with the energetic voices of an African gospel choir singing in Tswana about God and his goodness. While she wouldn't consider herself fluent in the language, she had picked up enough words over the years to understand what was being communicated. She opened her eyes to see that it was 05:00. It was already light in their room but sunrise was still an hour away.

She slowly rose from the thin mattress and slid off the bed, trying not to wake Maia. She tiptoed to the door, where she grabbed her dressing-gown from the hook and wrapped it around herself.

The gospel song had come to an end and the host of the early morning show started talking, his cheery voice much too upbeat, she always decided, for this time of the morning. Rachel shuffled towards the light switch and turned it on, illuminating the dark room with a harsh fluorescent glare. Next she headed towards the two-plate stove and emptied two cups of maize meal into a pot. She added four cups of water from the faucet above the metal sink and then turned the heat on low.

With the porridge cooking in the background, Rachel opened the door to the bathroom and began to run some hot water into the tub. She quickly climbed out of her night clothes and stepped in while it was still running. Picking up a bar of soap, she washed herself briskly before rinsing away the suds. She splashed water over her face and then climbed out onto the thin bathmat, dried her body with the old blue towel that hung from the railing in the corner of the small room, and applied lotion to her skin.

Age and motherhood had taken their toll and, while she weighed only 5kg more than she'd weighed in her teens, her firm body was slowly beginning to lose its grip on the youthfulness that she had once taken for granted. Blemishes had started to appear on her dark skin. She looked down at her belly as she applied the lotion to the rough scar she had been left with when they'd cut Maia out of her.

Leaving the hot water in the tub, Rachel slipped into a pair of jeans, a shirt and a jersey, all hand-me-downs from Michelle. One of the perks of her job was that she was the same size as her employer, which meant that whenever Michelle cleared out her closet, Rachel had first claim on whatever was to be given away. Because of this she hadn't had to buy clothes for herself in years, sending the money she might have spent on those items back to her parents.

Rachel left the bathroom and, after checking on the porridge that bubbled lazily on the stove, she walked over to the bed and gently shook Maia.

'Come, girl, you can't sleep in today.'

Slowly the blanket started to move and Rachel watched as her daughter's sleepy face emerged from the covers. She gave a big yawn and sat up in bed, keeping her eyes closed. She was on the verge of lying back down again when Rachel chuckled – she understood the temptation all too well – and shook her again.

'Go to the bath and get ready for school. We'll have breakfast when I get back.'

Her eyes still closed, Maia nodded. She climbed out of bed and started walking slowly towards the bathroom. Rachel looked out the window. It was going to be a beautiful day. The birds were chirping in the tree outside. She took a quick glance into the bathroom. Still sleepy eyed, Maia was already sitting in the tub and beginning to splash water over herself. She looked up and smiled at her mother.

Rachel smiled back. 'I'll be back now,' she told her. 'Make sure you clean properly.'

She opened the door and quickly stepped outside into the chilly driveway that separated her living quarters from the main property. The brickwork was covered in dew that reflected in the morning light and, as Rachel hurried past the double-door garage to the main house, she reminded herself that she would need to clean the windows sometime that week. In the middle of the driveway was a large oak tree. In summer its branches were covered in heavy green leaves that provided shade and a place to sit when she had her lunch outdoors. The morning sun was just beginning to peek through the gaps in the foliage.

The first time Rachel had walked into the Jordaan house she had been left speechless and in awe. She had seen big houses in Maputo but they had been the homes of politicians and industry captains who had spent their lives building them up, not the ordinary homes of people who were the same age as her.

She ascended the stone steps to the front entrance. The dark wooden door was surrounded by stone cladding that made it look welcoming and defensive at the same time. Rachel took out her set of keys. First she unlocked the metal security gate, then the door. Its hinges creaked as she pushed it open and entered the house. The air was filled with the beeping of the alarm system about to go off and she quickly punched the access code into the keypad on the wall next to the intercom.

Her early starting time was part of her working arrangement with the Jordaans, one that allowed her to take Maia to school between 6.30 and 8.00, if she was willing to start the laundry cycle and get the dishes done before then.

Rachel looked down to see Hugo, the strange looking dog the Jordaans had brought home last month, looking up at her with expectant eyes and a wagging tail. She shook her head and smiled at him, using her foot to keep him back while she turned on the lights to the entrance so that she could see her way down the dark passage. The wall in the passage was crowded with canvas prints of the Jordaans on their wedding day, sun-drenched images that showed younger versions of her employers in various poses that had been arranged to show their love for each other. Apparently they had hired one of the best photographers in South Africa to document their wedding; there was a glossy book with matching images on display in the living room showing everything that happened on the day, from the preparations to the reception. Occasionally, when the Jordaans were away and Rachel found herself waiting for the washing machine to finish its load, she would page through the book and stare at the beautiful photos of her employers. They looked like the models she saw staring back at her from the covers of the magazines at the store. Sometimes she wondered if she would look as beautiful in a wedding dress.

Rachel went through to the kitchen, Hugo scampering behind her, and opened the blinds. Morning light filled the room as she turned on the espresso machine and put the kettle on to boil. There was a puddle of urine on the tiled floor next to Hugo's basket. She shook her head as she bent down to clean up the mess with some paper towels. It had been like this every morning since the dog had arrived; she was grateful, at least, that she was dealing with a small animal. She knew that Hugo would not leave her side until he was fed and so she took out the bag of pellets and dished the correct amount, as Chris had shown her, into a plastic bowl and placed it on the floor to the side of the sink. Hugo immediately sank his face into it.

Rachel began to rinse the dirty plates and utensils from the previous night's meal before stacking them into the dishwasher. Out of all the chores that life as a domestic worker required her to do, washing dishes was the one she minded the least. She found the warm water comforting and the gentle scrubbing of the plates and cups cathartic. It was a task that was simple and yielded immediate results; the cleaning of what had once been dirty. Michelle preferred her to use the dishwasher, however, so now she stacked the machine, added a dishwashing tablet and hit the button that started the washing cycle. Looking up at the large clock on the wall, she saw that it was 05:50 and, after putting some coffee mugs on top of the warm espresso machine, she returned to her room.

She opened the door and found Maia sitting at the table with a spoon in her hand, dressed and ready for breakfast. Rachel gave her daughter a smile and closed the door behind her. She lifted the pot from the cooker and dished the white porridge into their bowls. She placed one of the bowls in front of Maia and passed her the sugar, watching her closely. Maia loved sugar and would always try to sneak in a few extra spoons when Rachel wasn't looking.

'One spoon, Maia,' she said automatically.

Maia put the spoon that was already armed with a second portion back into the sugar bowl and started to stir the hot porridge. She lifted a spoonful to her mouth when Rachel stopped her.

'Careful, it's hot.'

Maia stopped and blew on the porridge, small breaths that directed the steam away from the spoon. A few seconds passed and Maia stopped blowing. She looked enquiringly up at her mother.

'Can I eat now?' she asked in Portuguese.

'Only if you ask me in English.'

Rachel had decided the previous year that English would be Maia's first language, believing that the right accent and comprehension of the tongue would open up doors in her future that an African one wouldn't. It had been difficult to get Maia to switch over from Portuguese but the task became much easier when she had started attending nursery school. All the other children there spoke English.

'Can I eat now?' Maia asked again, this time in English.

Rachel frowned. 'Where did your manners go?'

The little girl took a deep breath and prepared herself to ask the question a third time.

'Can I eat now, pleeeease?'

Rachel laughed and nodded.

'Yes, you may.'

They began to eat their porridge and by the time the radio clock read 06:20 they were finished and standing at the doorway, the bowls washed and stacked in the drying rack. On her shoulders Maia had a bright pink, second-hand Barbie backpack that a friend of Chris's had given her. Rachel was wearing one of Michelle's old jackets.

'Do you have everything?'

Maia nodded and mother and daughter left the room they called home, using the side gate at the top of the driveway to exit the property and start their two kilometre walk to Maia's nursery school.

Michelle lay in the king-size bed she shared with Chris, her eyes closed as she listened to the slow rhythm of her husband's breathing beneath the duvet. Were it not for that sound she would have no way of telling if he was alive. During their first year of marriage she had often woken up in the middle of the night to check that his motionless body was still breathing. She had always been a light sleeper and it had taken her a while to get accustomed to the reality of sharing a bed with another person, even if that person slept like the dead.

Michelle was accustomed to going to bed late and rising early. Her work as a brand specialist demanded it. Her company's offices were in Sandton, the financial heart of Johannesburg, and she handled an account for one of the country's largest telecommunications companies, where she oversaw millions of rands in marketing expenditure. She knew the needs of the client inside out and prided herself on the fact that she was the first port of call for all major decisions made by the team.

Michelle picked up her iPhone and activated the screen, peering through foggy eyes at the bright display which told her that it was 06:28. She had two minutes before the alarm went off and she stretched her arms out as far as they would extend in an attempt to wake herself. As she lay beside him she watched Chris as he slept, taking in the tiny details that could only be learned through time and proximity. What had once been smile lines in the corners of his eyes were now the beginning of wrinkles and, as she looked at the side of his head, she could see the first streaks of grey that had started to appear that year. He was ageing well, though, his boyish good looks gradually being replaced with a distinguished façade. She reached over and tickled his arm softly.

'Wakey, wakey, *liefie*.'

Chris moved slowly, his body responding to her touch as he groaned and retreated deeper under the warm duvet.

'What time is it?' he asked without opening his eyes.

'Six-thirty.'

Michelle leaned into him, kissing him on his exposed shoulder before starting to nuzzle his neck, the sensation causing him to tense up and laugh as he tried to resist. Michelle didn't stop and eventually Chris sat up abruptly, pushing her away. They were both laughing.

'Stop!' Chris said, holding Michelle back before pulling her in again and wrapping his arms around her. He returned the neck nuzzle, armed with morning stubble, and Michelle screamed out in laughter and protest. Chris stopped but pulled his wife's body towards his as they lay back on the bed. Michelle tried to sit up but Chris pulled her back down, the duvet doing little to hide his intentions.

'No...' Michelle laughed.

'Come on,' Chris said. 'It's early still. You know I only need about five minutes.'

Michelle sat up and looked down at him. Chris's eyes were wide, innocent, but a naughty smile flickered across his face.

'You know we only hit my fertility window tomorrow and – '

Chris cut her off by trying to pull her towards him again but Michelle fended him off with her hands.

' – the doctor said that you need to control yourself to increase your – '

'Don't say it!'

' – your ...'

'Michelle! You know I hate it when you talk like that.'

Michelle laughed and pretended to stop, waiting for Chris to let his guard down before she shouted out the last two words.

' – sperm count!'

Chris put his hands over his ears, trying to block the words out before turning on Michelle and pulling her firmly towards him, tickling her for good measure. Michelle lay still, with a look of defiance in her eyes, desperately trying to resist the sensation until she couldn't any more. She burst out laughing. Chris stopped tickling her and, holding her arms down, brought his face closer to hers. He kissed her softly on her lips.

'No,' Michelle said.

'Please.'

'No.'

'Come on.'

'No.'

'Just the tip,' Chris said. 'You won't even know I was there.'

'You're disgusting!' Michelle laughed and pushed him away. 'Go do something useful and get us some coffee.'

'Fine!' Chris slumped down in the bed, accepting the fact that his early morning attempt at seduction was going to be unsuccessful today. Michelle watched as he climbed out of bed, his red boxer shorts unable to hide the fact that he had indeed been ready to go. Chris saw her looking at him and turned to face her, his erection poking through the slit in the underwear.

'Last chance.'

Michelle reached for the pillow behind her head and threw it at him, narrowly missing the mirror he was standing next to.

'Coffee!'

As Chris's heavy footsteps faded away down the passage to the kitchen and the bedroom returned to silence, Michelle closed her eyes. Her thoughts were racing and she urged them to be still. Even though they had been joking around, she and Chris both knew that the next day was going to be serious.

She placed her hands on her stomach and started to whisper prayers over her womb, begging God and urging her body to repair the parts that were not working.

Chris held the door open for Michelle while she collected her keys from the rack and picked up her laptop, handbag and an umbrella. It didn't look as though it would rain but he knew how she always liked to be prepared. He smiled to himself as he thought about his wife's eccentricities, her need for things to be organised and the contrast that his way of living brought to that.

Theirs had been a case of opposites attracting, that was for sure.

Even in the cool of the courtyard Chris could tell it was going to be a warm day. The smell of the previous night's brief thunderstorm was still fresh on the grass. He smiled at his wife as she walked through the open door and as he prepared to close it behind her he saw Rachel coming down the path towards them.

'Morning, Rachel.'

'Good morning, Chris. Morning, Michelle,' Rachel replied, walking a little faster to meet her employers.

'Hey!' Michelle smiled warmly at Rachel as she strolled towards her grey Audi TT, struggling to juggle her bags. 'There are some croissants in the bread bin, if you want, and I've left some clothes on the counter if you want anything before I send them to the church.'

'Thank you,' Rachel said. She reached out to help Michelle with her bags.

'*Ag, dankie*, Rachel,' Michelle said, handing the laptop case to her. 'Oh, and we're going to dinner straight after work, so please would you lock up and put the alarm on when you're done for the day?'

Rachel nodded, smiling.

Michelle turned to kiss Chris goodbye.

'And this?' he joked, kissing her back.

'Can you pick up a bottle of red after work, Chris? I'm not going to have time to get to the shops after my meeting.'

‘Text me later to remind me. Where are we going again?’

‘It’s Karlien’s 30th and she’s having an 80s party, which means I need you to swing past the party shop to pick up our costumes too.’

‘Got it. What are we going as?’

‘I told you already,’ Michelle said, letting go of his collar.

‘Remind me.’

‘I’m going as Cyndi Lauper and you’re going as …’

‘Marty McFly!’ Chris interrupted her. ‘How could I forget? Did you get me my – ’

‘Hoverboard?’ Michelle said, returning the interruption as she opened the trunk. With a flamboyant gesture she pulled out a skateboard deck that was missing its wheels. ‘All sorted.’

Chris grinned and kissed Michelle on the lips.

‘You’re pretty cool, you know.’

‘I know, *lief*.’

Michelle fixed his collar and, when she was done, Chris opened her car door for her. Michelle climbed inside and Chris stepped back so that she could reverse out of the driveway. Rachel was still standing at the bottom of the steps to the front door, waiting for them to leave. Michelle put the Audi in gear and then she rolled down her window.

‘Have a good day, Rachel!’ she called out. ‘And thanks for putting on the espresso machine for us this morning.’

Chris got into his own car and started the engine. The sound of John Mayer’s Paradise Valley filled the space as his sound system came to life. As he reversed up the driveway, he gave Rachel a wave before backing out into the suburban street and joining the throng of commuters in the Johannesburg traffic.

Chris worked at one of the city’s most prestigious architectural firms, one that was specialising in the rejuvenation of large buildings in four of South Africa's key cities: Johannesburg, Pretoria, Durban and Cape Town. He was busy overseeing multiple projects in all four cities but the ones that excited him the most were those happening closest to home. The city of Johannesburg had undergone a renaissance of sorts over the last ten years, with areas that had been derelict and filled with crime now occupied by hipsters, coffee shops and businesses. People were returning to the city they used to fear and Chris believed that in some small way the buildings he was helping renovate were contributing to this rebirth. He actually wished that he and Michelle could live in the CBD rather than the suburbs but Michelle had made it very clear that she would not set foot in downtown Joburg. She still held fast to many of the valid fears from the past. The irony was that Chris was more comfortable leaving his car unattended in the streets of the CBD than in the ones outside his house. It was his view that most of the criminals came to the suburbs when they wanted to do their shopping. The high walls, electric fences, alarm systems and security guards that filled their neighbourhood provided an illusion of safety but, in his opinion, would do little to keep danger out if it decided to come looking.

As the car filled with blues riffs, his thoughts drifted to Rachel and the years she had spent working for him and Michelle. The three of them had lived on the same property for quite a few years now – at least five, he thought, if not six – but he didn't know all that much about her. He considered himself a friendly person and had gone out of his way to get to know her – where she came from and what she wanted from life – but there was always a wall, a distance, that she kept between them and which time had not changed. He despised the 'old way' that he had grown up with, the one where domestic workers were just maids, anonymous entities that cleaned during the day and disappeared at sunset. He had always promised himself that if he were ever to employ someone to take care of domestic work in his home, he would treat her as he would a co-worker or a friend.

He had just never factored in the idea that the desire might not be reciprocated.

By now he had left the suburban roads and was manoeuvring the car onto William Nicol, the congested four-lane road that led into Sandton. The traffic was slowly inching forward when, out of the corner of his eye, he noticed movement in the car alongside him. Looking to his right, he saw a pretty auburn-haired woman with a big smile on her face waving at him. It took a few moments for him to recognise that it was the new PA from the office. He couldn't remember her name but he raised his hand and returned the greeting. Unable to talk to each other, the woman made a frustrated face while pointing to the traffic ahead of them and Chris rolled his eyes in agreement. He ran a finger across his throat and the woman laughed. Chris laughed too and then, both of them unsure how to continue their silent conversation, he waved goodbye and turned his attention back to the road. For the next 30 minutes or so he was conscious of their cars keeping pace beside each other and that both of them were studiously pretending the other wasn't there.

Eventually, Chris put his sunglasses on and turned up his music, but he was too aware of himself to sing along to the songs as he usually did on his way in to work. He could have sworn he could see the woman glancing his way a few times, but he acted as though he didn't notice.

Rachel stood assessing the mess in the kitchen that had been left for her to deal with by the Jordaans after their breakfast. Actually, it wasn't too bad today. There were only a few bowls and two coffee cups. After stacking them in the dishwasher, she switched on the kettle to make herself some tea. She looked inside the bread bin for the croissants Michelle had told her would be there. There were two there and she took them out and cut them in half, squashing them flat so that they would fit inside the toaster. Even though Chris had shown her how to use the microwave she still had a healthy disdain for the machine after the only meal she'd tried to heat in it had exploded. Chris had told her that it was because she had used a metal container but the memory of the sparks inside the microwave left her with little desire to use it again.

Hugo was looking up at her expectantly and Rachel opened the door to the garden, shooing the dog out so that she could have her breakfast in peace. She dropped a teabag into one of the Jordaans' heavy coffee mugs and poured hot water over it, smelling the fragrant herbs as their scent wafted up towards her nose. The toaster ejected the croissants and, after buttering and layering them with jam, she took a seat at the small wooden table in the breakfast nook at the far end of the kitchen.

In the daily routine of her life, this was the moment when Rachel would pause and gather her thoughts, the moment when everything around her was still.

As she took her first sip of tea she looked across the table and through the large glass sliding doors into the beautiful garden behind the house. It was immaculately landscaped. The grass was perfectly manicured and the flowerbeds were planted at even intervals with lavender bushes in shades of purple and silver. In the centre of the lawn was a large rectangular swimming pool with one of those walls that wasn't a wall but dropped away to nothingness – an infinity pool, Chris had told her this design was called – with a view out over the northern side of the city. The view was truly spectacular and Rachel often sat on the steps at the back door at dusk before the Jordaans came home from work, watching the lights of the city come on.

Chris and Michelle only ever seemed to use the swimming pool when they had people over. For the most part it was merely decorative.

As she sat sipping her tea Rachel saw Richmond, the Zimbabwean gardener, throw a cup of chlorine into the crystal waters. Richmond saw her and waved, mouthing hello to her in English before returning his attention to the water that he kept so beautifully clean and clear. His home language was Ndebele but he did have a sprinkling of rather poor English, too, which meant that the latter had become their language of choice when it came to he and Rachel communicating with each other. Richmond had been with the Jordaans longer than she had. His days were Tuesdays, Thursdays and Saturdays, and his duties were to cut the grass, clean the pool and do any yard work that the property required. Rachel would make him lunch on those days but they generally kept to themselves, largely due, she supposed, to the language barrier.

For a few minutes Rachel watched the white powder falling into the water. Then she closed her eyes, choosing instead to picture the salty waters and the deep blue ocean she had grown up beside. The water here was dead, blue only because of the chemicals that probably hurt your eyes and made your skin dry. And even with all the chemicals Richmond put into the infinity pool, the colour of the water didn't compare to the vibrant shades of blue of the Bazaruto

Archipelago. For Rachel the swimming pool was a symbol for the existence that she witnessed in the Johannesburg suburbs – beautiful and clean but devoid of life and colour.

Lately Maia had been pestering Rachel to teach her how to swim and she had promised she would, but not until she was six. She'd told her she would have to be patient and wait until the December holidays when the Jordaans usually went away on vacation. They'd stayed home this summer and Rachel was quite relieved. The real reason for delaying the lessons was the simple fact that she could not swim herself. Somehow she would have to learn before she could teach Maia. Perhaps Chris would help. Even though she had grown up next to the sea, swimming was something the tourists and some fishermen did, and she had never had the desire to venture further in to the water than knee deep. It seemed that most of the children at Maia's nursery school already knew how to swim. They had probably all grown up with pools in their own back yards, perhaps even similar to the infinity pool she was looking at now.

Taking one last sip of her tea, Rachel got to her feet and prepared herself for the tasks of the day.

chapter 3

RACHEL STOOD IN the kitchen with a piece of paper in her hand, reading through the list of chores that had been left for her to complete. Her four weeks of absence had resulted in a load of work that could not feasibly be done in one day and so she resigned herself to the fact that the week ahead was going to be a difficult one.

During the time she had been away, the normal clutter in the Jordaan house had multiplied alarmingly. The list bore the clean lines and penmanship that belonged to Michelle but, when she turned the paper over, the note on the other side had clearly been written by Chris. In a decidedly untidy script, it said: *Welcome back Rachel. We had to get to the doctor for an appointment but this list will tell you everything that needs to be done. Your wages are in the envelope. Chris & Michelle.*

Rachel picked up the envelope where it lay on the kitchen counter and opened it. The R100 notes were neatly stacked. She didn't need to count them to know they added up to her monthly wage of R4 500, by South African standards a very good wage, considering that all of her living expenses and Maia's nursery school fees were covered by the Jordaans. They had always been generous employers and it was because of this quality that she had been able to not only support her parents back in Mozambique but also save about R200 every month, if there weren't any emergencies.

But now their generosity felt tainted, the money that she was holding soaked in compromise.

Out of long habit, Rachel switched on the kettle and, as she waited for the water to boil, began to rinse the precariously toppling pile of dishes in the sink and stack them in the dishwasher. It looked like every item of cutlery and crockery the Jordaans owned was in that sink, while a pile of take-away cartons and pizza boxes next to the trashcan in the corner of the kitchen bore testimony to the meals they'd been eating recently.

She started the first load and then poured boiling water from the kettle into her mug, opening the bread bin at the same time to see if there was anything there for her to eat. With her routine now broken, she had found herself skipping breakfast lately, opting to lie in bed for an extra 30 minutes in the morning. The bread bin was empty. She wasn't really disappointed. She'd pretty much lost her appetite along with her routine. When she did eat it was because she knew she needed to and not because she was hungry.

Taking her customary seat at the table in the breakfast nook, Rachel looked out at the garden as she always did. Winter was definitely on the way. The grass was still green but this was more due to Richmond's watering three times a week than defiance of the season. Soon the garden would turn to shades of brown and yellow, colours that would contrast vividly with the blue of the highveld sky in winter.

Rachel was not looking forward to another season of cold. She watched a golden leaf disconnect from the oak tree that had once been its life source and flutter slowly downwards, where it joined a scattering of other leaves on the surface of the swimming pool. Where before the pool had been as clear as crystal it now had a tinge of green. She remembered Chris explaining this to her once, how it always happened after a lot of rain and also when the seasons changed.

As they waited in Dr Pieterse's office, Michelle checked the time on her iPhone and then looked across at Chris, who was sitting in the chair next to hers. He winked at her and she gave him a small smile. She had just had her very first ultrasound and Michelle could feel the residue of the clear jelly that Dr Pieterse had applied to her still flat belly before moving the wand across it. When the fuzzy grey image had appeared on the monitor next to them, Dr Pieterse had checked the heartbeat, position, size and breathing of the baby, while Chris took photos. He wanted to save these for their announcement on social media later that day.

While they had told their parents, a couple of close friends, and his work colleagues, they still hadn't made it 'Facebook official' and had decided to wait until after the first scan to do this. Chris wanted to announce it in an original way. They had been toying with the idea of uploading a photo of a bread roll baking in an oven or just the ultrasound photo by itself. Chris had taken the mandatory selfie of the two of them while the scan was happening and Michelle had put on a smile, even though she hadn't been feeling great.

She hadn't specifically timed their appointment with Rachel's first day back but Chris would have preferred that they were there in person to welcome her. Still, the excuse was a valid one for them to be out of the house and he could tell Michelle was relieved.

Michelle put her iPhone away and looked across the desk at Dr Pieterse, who was busy with an urgent phone call from one of her other patients. As Michelle listened to the doctor dispense advice over the phone, she wondered if she would end up being one of those patients who called her gynae constantly with every fear and false alarm. Dr Pieterse apologised to Michelle and Chris with her eyes as she continued her conversation, aware that the call was intruding on their appointment. She was one of the top gynaecologists in Johannesburg, operating from the Sandton Mediclinic, and her patience with the woman on the phone reassured Michelle that she was in good and caring hands. She had been going to Dr Pieterse for a few years now and she trusted her. She had walked them through the emotional and physical minefields that face couples who struggle to conceive. Michelle watched her as she started to finish up the conversation, her professional façade always present. The thought occurred to her suddenly that she was sharing a room with the two people who knew her body inside out, one as lover and the other as healer.

'Sorry about that,' Dr Pieterse said as she hung up and turned to face Michelle and Chris. She picked up their file and began scanning through the notes she had made earlier. 'I know you've been waiting for this baby for a long time so I'm going to be honest with you,' she said. 'I'm concerned about the baby's heartbeat. It is a bit weak and your blood pressure, Michelle, is far too high.'

Michelle took in the information, waiting for Dr Pieterse to continue.

'Unfortunately, medication is not an option so we're going to have to try and find ways of adjusting your lifestyle to assist in this. How are things at work?'

'Work? It's busy but that's marketing for you.'

'A lot of stress?'

'No more than anyone else's job.'

'Look, high blood pressure is often related to stress levels, and diet as well. Given your age and the data I have here, you're going to need to cut down on work.'

'What do you mean? Work half-days?'

Michelle couldn't quite grasp what she was being told. She let go of Chris's hand and leaned forward, waiting for Dr Pieterse to get to the point. The doctor paused. She seemed to be trying to figure out how best to tell her patient what she needed to hear.

'I mean stop working all together.'

Michelle sat back and tried to process the information, the shock causing her to go silent. Six months of not working? Where some people might jump at the idea of six months of house rest, for her this would be nothing less than a prison sentence. She looked over at Chris who had started to chuckle. He was busy trying to explain to Dr Pieterse why stopping work was not going to be a good idea for his wife at all.

'You clearly haven't met my wife, Dr Pieterse,' Chris said, placing his hand on Michelle's shoulder. 'This is the woman who took her laptop with her on our honeymoon. To Mauritius.'

Dr Pieterse didn't laugh.

'I don't think my job is the problem,' Michelle protested. 'I know plenty of women who work until eight months with no problem. I can't just stop *working*.'

'Michelle, do you want to have this baby?'

'Of course I do. What kind of a ques – '

'Then having this baby is going to be your job now. Your full-time job for the next six months.' The doctor's tone left Michelle in no doubt that what she was saying was not a suggestion.

'And I can't even drink coffee anymore,' Michelle said, frustration dripping from each word.

They were sitting at one of the wooden tables at The Whippet, a trendy cafe nestled in the heart of the suburb of Linden.

Chris took a self-aware sip of his Americano. He knew his wife was waiting for a response from him and he needed to choose his words carefully. When Michelle was in this zone she always looked for someone to argue with and when she couldn't do it with the person she was actually angry with, she would find a way to use Chris as a verbal punching bag.

'Why don't I get you some fruit juice? Or a bottle of water?' Chris suggested tentatively.

'You know I hate drinking water.'

Chris sighed and picked up the menu, scanning what was on offer so that he wouldn't have to carry on with the conversation, but he could feel Michelle glaring at him. He glanced up at her and registered immedifately that, as he'd suspected, his wife was unimpressed by the fact that he wasn't engaging with her on the matter.

'What?' Chris said and Michelle shook her head at him.

'What are we going to do? You know we need both our salaries to make it through the month. There's no way my company will give me paid leave for that long.'

'I don't know,' Chris replied, putting the menu down. 'I'm sure we'll find a way to make it work.'

'That's a great attitude,' Michelle fumed, sitting back in her chair.

The waitress approached the table and asked if she could get them anything to eat. Chris looked over at Michelle, who pointedly ignored the question. He ordered a bacon and egg tramezzini and handed the menus to the waitress. Then he looked at Michelle again. He could see how her emotions were swirling below the surface and he tried to imagine what she was going through. Looking down, he noticed the grey dog that had inspired the name of the cafe weaving its way through the tables, dodging busy waiters and looking for a customer willing to part with scraps from their plate.

'I think Dr Pieterse was pretty clear,' Chris said, his tone gentle and empathetic.

He waited to hear the pebble hit the water. He watched Michelle's face carefully. When she looked up at him, her eyes were glistening with the tears that she refused to let fall.

'It's easy to say when you're not the one who has to do it,' Michelle replied. She was making an effort to keep her voice steady.

'Don't make it like that.'

Michelle looked away. Chris leaned forward, placing his hands on her knees in an attempt to break through the wall she was putting up and allow her to see his heart.

'We'll find things to help you pass the time,' he told her. 'We'll –'

But his sentence was cut off as the waitress arrived with his food. Chris thanked her and as soon as the plate was in front of him began vigorously to apply salt to his tramezzini. 'Are you sure you're not hungry?' he asked.

Michelle shook her head.

Chris picked up one of the warm slices and took a large bite. Michelle was right; they couldn't live the way they were living on just his salary. The truth was that Michelle had always earned the higher salary and, while Chris had never had a problem with this as far as his pride was concerned, he could see how they had worked themselves into a tight corner. If Michelle was physically unable to earn a living ...

But money, Chris knew, wasn't going to be the only problem.

Rachel hadn't come up in their conversation yet, but he knew that she was part of the reason for Michelle being against the idea of being house bound. While he couldn't blame her for feeling the way she did, he also couldn't think of how to find a way around it. They could not fire Rachel and they definitely wouldn't be able to support her if they hired another maid to take her place.

His iPhone beeped as he took another bite. He checked the message. It was from one of his colleagues at work. He smiled while he thought of a suitably clever response.

'I'll let work know tomorrow,' Michelle said gloomily.

Chris glanced up briefly from his phone, his thumbs still typing, and nodded.

'I'll have to wrap up the French campaign before I hand it over but I'll tell them I'll work on that from home.'

Rachel looked around the clean kitchen one last time and then at the clock on the wall. It was 5pm. She had been waiting all day for the front door to open so that she could get through her first encounter with Michelle, and yet here she was still, anticipating that awkward moment with increasing anxiety. With little more to do now, she decided to go to her room. She turned on the lights in the passage, locked the security gate and front door behind her, and started walking up the path towards the driveway.

A glance into the courtyard as she went past reminded her that she had forgotten to bring the trashcans in from the street. She hurried up the driveway to the side gate. The two large trashcans, which had been emptied earlier that day by the municipality, were propped against the pavement. The Jordaans lived at the end of a street that was boomed off for security and the entrance to the neighbourhood was protected by a security guard at all times. The road was lined with old jacaranda trees whose purple flowers transformed the neighbourhood when they heralded the arrival of spring, a look they'd discarded a while back. Rachel reached the trashcans and was about to roll them back inside when she heard a voice behind her.

'And?'

She smiled and turned at the familiar voice.

'Hello, Maria,' she greeted her friend. 'I didn't see you there.'

Maria was from Malawi and she worked for the family who lived next door to the Jordaans. Loud and built like tank, she was the polar opposite to Tapiwa, the thin woman who was standing next to her. Tapiwa came from Zimbabwe and she worked a few houses to the left of the Jordaans. She usually let Maria do all of the talking. As with Richmond and Rachel, English ended up being the common language among the three women, but time and familiarity had resulted in the transfer of certain phrases from each of their first languages. The mixture was comfortable and they were easy in their communication.

The three friends strolled together to the corner of the street, where they sat down on the grass that grew between the road and the high walls of the properties. If drinking tea in the Jordaans' kitchen or having her lunch outdoors beneath the oak tree was how she routinely spent her alone time, then sitting on the grass on the corner of the street with Maria and Tapiwa was Rachel's evening socialising.

Like most domestic workers in South Africa, they were not permitted to invite friends onto the properties where they lived due to the security risks this access posed to their employers. The next best place for them to gather was on the grass outside the houses where they worked and they would sit there in their uniforms and gossip about the events of the day until the sun disappeared and they were forced by the darkness to return to their respective domestic quarters.

Rachel lay on her stomach, while Maria and Tapiwa sat in front of her, the fading afternoon sunlight warming them as they listened to the cars hum past. The afternoon rush was about 30 minutes deep.

'And?' Tapiwa echoed Maria's question. 'How was your first day back?'

'They were out the whole time.'

Maria chuckled. 'So it was good.'

'There was a lot to do.' Rachel sighed, rubbing her tired eyes. 'I don't think they cleaned the place at all while I was away.'

'They probably don't even know where the dishwashing liquid is,' Maria said and the other women laughed because they knew the joke was probably true.

They were still laughing when they heard the electric gate to the Jordaans' property open and watched as Chris's Z4 stopped while he waited for the gate to slide slowly open before he could turn into the driveway. As Chris lowered his window Rachel pushed herself up so that she could speak to her employer. She saw Michelle in the passenger seat, her sunglasses shielding her eyes. She was looking steadfastly in the opposite direction. She wondered what had happened during the day to put her in such a mood.

'Hey, Rachel,' Chris said, pulling her attention from Michelle to him. 'I'm sorry we couldn't be here this morning to welcome you back. How did it go?'

'Everything is clean, Mr Jordaan,' Rachel replied.

Chris looked a bit taken aback at the unusual formality, but the electric gate had finished opening so, raising a hand, he eased the car forward to get through the gate before it closed on him. While some of the electric security gates had sensors that stopped the gate from closing if an object was in its way, the Jordaans had opted to get one that closed regardless, believing that if they were ever held up, it would be better if the hijackers were unable to stop the gate from closing.

Rachel watched the car disappearing down the driveway until it was out of sight. Then she returned her attention to Maria and Tapiwa, who were both watching her, trying to read her emotion. The three women sat in silence for a few moments.

Then Rachel spoke.

'She's pregnant,' she said quietly.

'What?!?' Maria and Tapiwa both exclaimed.

Rachel nodded, but chose not to say anything more. They were all silent, their eyes on the road and the fancy cars driving past in a long slow line.

'It makes me sick,' Maria said after a while.

'What does?' Rachel asked.

'To see you cleaning up after those people.'

'It is what it is, Maria.'

'I know,' Maria replied 'but it still makes me sick.'

Rachel sighed and picked up a dry twig from the grass. She began to snap it into smaller pieces as she contemplated her situation. Maria and Tapiwa watched as she tossed the pieces to the side.

'My purse is too light for me to be proud,' Rachel said eventually, as she threw the last piece of the twig to the ground.

Michelle strode into the house ahead of Chris, taking off her sunglasses so that she could inspect the place. First walking through to the kitchen, she saw that the mess of the last few weeks had disappeared and had been replaced by order and cleanliness. A quick stroll through the rest of the house revealed that the rooms had been vacuumed, the bed had been made and that the large pile of laundry had been washed, ironed and folded.

Finally, Michelle thought, *a bit of sanity.*

On her way back to the kitchen she saw Chris's tie and work shoes on the passage floor but she ignored them. She found her husband at the fridge, a beer in his hand. She watched him take a sip from the bottle and go over to the breakfast nook.

'At least the house is back in order,' Michelle said as she opened the fridge to see what they could have for dinner. When Chris didn't answer, she looked up from the shelves and saw that he was staring out the window at the swimming pool as the last rays of sun bathed their garden.

'You could have greeted her when we drove in,' Chris said, not turning away from the view.

Michelle closed the fridge and spoke to his back.

'I didn't see she was there until we were halfway down the driveway.'

She waited for Chris to challenge her feeble excuse but nothing came. He just took another sip of his beer and continued to stare out the window. She watched as he set the bottle down on the wooden table and saw the beads of condensation slide onto the bleached wood. She pushed a coaster towards him and Chris turned his head slightly. Slowly he picked up the beer and put it on the coaster.

Michelle opened the fridge again and pulled out a ready-made Chicken Pesto meal from Woolworths.

'Can I help?'

'I've got it.'

'Cool.'

Michelle heard the kitchen door open.

'Where are you going?' she asked, turning quickly.

'I want to test the water in the pool. It's looking a little off.'

'Oh.'

Michelle went back to assembling their evening meal. For weeks now her body had been feeling strange, as though all of her senses were heightened and overriding her rational mind. What she could only describe as waves of saturation would move through her, leaving her lightheaded and, of all emotions, teary. She hated crying. She had worn her sunglasses all the way home, just in case.

The news from Dr Pieterse had not helped her already fragile state of mind.

She had wanted this baby for so long and, now that it was here, she wished she could be more excited about what was happening. So much had changed since she had first found out she was pregnant. She couldn't help but wonder if things would be better if the baby just wasn't there.

She couldn't imagine what Rachel must be thinking, knowing that she was expecting. The irony of it all had not escaped Michelle but for the last few weeks she had managed to push whatever guilt she was feeling behind a shroud of busyness and work. But now, trapped in a space where she would be forced to be still, she couldn't ignore the voice that was screaming in her mind, calling her name and demanding her attention.

Chris fished around the wooden shed at the bottom of the garden, pushing past spider webs as he looked for the testing kit. He found the dusty container between the chemicals and garden tools and took it to the side of the pool where he began preparations for the tests. Kneeling down, he scooped up some water from the cold pool and added a drop of chlorine neutraliser and five drops of red solution to test the PH levels. This he followed by adding another solution to read the acid levels. While he waited for the colours to settle, he picked up the indicator chart to compare the readings.

Nothing seemed out of the ordinary on the charts but the pool was definitely looking off colour. Shaking his head, he tossed the test water into the pool and took the kit back to the shed. If he was honest, Chris didn't know much about maintaining a swimming pool but it was early in the season for it to be going this murky colour. He decided he would test it again tomorrow and hope for a stronger reading. If push came to shove he could call in a professional but something inside of him wanted to handle this himself. His father had always taken care of these things when he was a boy and he wanted to prove that he could do the same.

He was about to walk back to the house when a message came through on his phone. He dug his cell out of his pocket and saw that he had a friend request on Facebook. He opened the app. It was from Anja, the redhead in his office. He smiled at the fact that she had been first to initiate the connection. Not wanting to appear too eager, he delayed accepting the request. Instead he scanned through her profile again and saw from one of her photographs that she had just completed a hike in the Drakensberg with a group of friends – #topofthemountain.

He heard Michelle call out from the kitchen and saw her silhouette moving back and forth against the window. Supper must be ready.

Chris hit 'ACCEPT', shoved the phone back in his pocket and walked back to the house.

Michelle woke with a start. Disorientated, her heart pounding, she pushed herself onto her elbows and looked around the dark bedroom. What was that *noise*? Frantically, she shook Chris's arm until he woke up, grumbling sleepily.

'What's wrong?' he mumbled. 'Michelle?'

'There's something outside,' Michelle hissed at him. 'Listen. It's like ... like screaming. Can't you *hear* it, Chris?'

Michelle stared fixedly at the curtained window, not moving. Chris half sat up and listened, trying to identify what it was she was hearing. Then suddenly he got it. He flopped back down on his pillow and began to pull the duvet back up over him.

'What?' Michelle said. 'Why aren't you – '

'It's just the pool cleaner, Michelle,' he told her, sighing irritably.

'Are you sure?' Michelle still seemed to be expecting him to do something. 'I've never heard it do that before,' she added accusingly.

'Of course you have,' Chris said, fluffing his pillow and getting ready to go back to sleep. 'It happens when it gets stuck in the corner of the pool and gets too close to the surface. Just give it five minutes and it'll fall back into the water.'

Michelle wasn't satisfied with his response and kept glaring at him, annoyed that he was clearly not planning on doing anything about it and, worse, was about to fall peacefully into his habitual deep sleep. Already his breathing was slowing. She resisted the urge to shake him.

The screaming sound grew in intensity, the cold air causing it to travel through the house like a banshee.

She hated that infinity pool.

They had been drawn to the idea of it when they were looking to purchase a home but when the reality of owning a swimming pool settled in, she realised that they didn't use it enough to warrant the upkeep and hassle. It was nothing but a giant water feature which, if it hadn't been for Richmond, would have turned into a green cesspool ages ago. Last year they had even considered filling it in and turning it into a deck but in the end Chris had said he wanted their children to grow up with a pool to play in and she had accepted his reasoning.

Chris had fond childhood memories of waiting for his father to come home from work so that he and his brothers could swim with their dad. He looked forward to the day when he'd be doing the same with his children. Chris's childhood summers had always been lived out in close proximity to an urban body of water. He told Michelle he'd be a selfish man if he got rid of theirs and deprived their future children just because it was proving to be hard work.

Michelle closed her eyes and waited for sleep to return, trying to push the awful sound from her mind.

Rachel lay in her bed, hugging the pillow to her stomach, wishing she could fall asleep. No matter how tightly she held onto the pillow, it still did not fill the space that Maia's small beating heart had once fit so perfectly.

The pool cleaner was stuck again. The shrill sucking, shrieking sound rang in her ears.

Maia had been gone for over six weeks and every night Rachel had woken up expecting to feel her child in front of her, Maia's shallow breathing pushing her back against Rachel's chest. It was the only moment Rachel lived for now, the one when, for the few seconds between sleeping and waking, her heart believed that Maia was still alive. It was in that space, before reason told her otherwise, that she felt complete. But then her brain would stir from its slumber and remind her of the truth, the truth that the child that she had created, the person who had grown inside of her, was gone forever.

She pushed her face deep into the pillow and began to weep,

bottomless cries that mixed with the wailing from the garden and faded into the cold night.

chapter 4

RACHEL, MARIA AND Tapiwa were sitting on the pavement, finding relief from the summer heat in the shade of a mulberry tree as they sorted through the bag of clothes Michelle had given Rachel. They had collected a few of the sweet purple berries and were enjoying the snack while trying to keep the scarlet juice from staining their clothes. Maria held one of the shirts against her chest; it was clearly too small for her.

'Designer, neh?'

Tapiwa laughed. Rachel sat back while her friends made their selections from the bag, depleting the stock quickly.

'Take something for Rita as well,' Rachel said, popping a mulberry into her mouth.

'Shame, she's lucky she's still here,' said Maria. She began to fan her face with a newspaper pamphlet that was advertising weekend specials at Game supermarket. 'They are becoming stricter on the Mozambicans now, do you know that, Rachel? They wanted a stamped letter from the Elliotts to say she works and lives with them.'

'How long did they give her?' Rachel asked.

'Six months.'

The women sat in contemplative silence for a few moments, eating their mulberries, hardly noticing the expensive cars of their neighbours driving past them.

'Rebecca was sent back last week,' Tapiwa said. 'The people she worked for moved to Cape Town and she couldn't find work before her visa ran out. The SAPD did a raid on the taxi rank she was at and when they saw that her papers had expired they put her in the van. Two days later she was at the border.'

'What?' Maria exclaimed. 'Didn't they give her a chance to get her stuff?'

Tapiwa shook her head and Maria muttered something under her breath in Chichewa.

'Where is her family?' Rachel asked.

'Inhassoro.'

'That is where my parents live. Things have not been good there for a long time.'

Rachel looked down at her cellphone and, when she saw the time, clambered to her feet and dusted the grass from her uniform.

'I need to go fetch Maia.'

'How is she doing at the rich school?' Maria chuckled.

'She's too young to understand.' Rachel smiled as she stretched. 'Shame, she tells them all about "our big house with the swimming pool" and how she's going to have a mermaid party for her birthday.'

'What's a mermaid?' Maria asked.

Rachel shrugged. 'Some girl who lives underneath the water, from the stories that the white people tell their children. She wants to learn to swim because of this mermaid thing now.'

Maria and Tapiwa laughed at the idea and they began to gather their things. The clock was telling them that they, too, needed to get back to work.

'God blessed you with a good family to work for,' Tapiwa said. 'You're the only maid I know whose boss pays for her child's school.'

Rachel pulled a face. 'Well, if you see the mess I have to clean up, you'd think they'd send her to university as well.'

The women went their separate ways and Rachel hurried to the side gate of the Jordaans' property. In her room she quickly changed out of her maid's uniform into the jeans and blue shirt she'd inherited from another of Michelle's clear-outs. She left the house at a pace that wouldn't have her drenched in sweat when she arrived at Maia's nursery school.

Where Maia had no idea that she was any different from the other boys and girls at Jollyjammers, Rachel did. That was why she never went to pick her daughter up in her maid's uniform. Like Father Christmas or the Easter Bunny for her white friends, Rachel wanted Maia to believe this fantasy for as long as she possibly could. She knew things would be different for Maia if the other mothers saw her as 'the maid's child'. And she'd be lying to herself if she didn't admit that it was good to be looked at as a person by the kind of people who usually only saw her as a function.

Rachel reached the nursery school ten minutes after the collection time, a strategy which she used to keep her from having to get too close to the other mothers. Conversations would lead to questions and questions would lead to the truth and, while she didn't want to be part of their world, she wanted them to think that she was.

'Look, Mama!'

Rachel followed the sound of Maia's voice and saw the little girl running from the school gate towards her, the pink backpack on her shoulders rocking back and forth. She knelt down to hug her and Maia jumped into her arms, excited to show her mother what she had in her hands.

It was a Barbie doll, like the one on Maia's backpack, with long blonde hair and bright blue eyes, but instead of slim, long legs this one had a fish's body that sparkled with blue and green scales, although closer inspection showed that some of the sparkle had worn off from handling. Rachel sighed and took the doll from Maia as she straightened up.

'You know you can't take the toys from school home with you,' she said.

'But it's not from school, Mama!' Maia protested. 'Abigail gave it to me!'

'Come, let's take it back.'

'But it's mine!'

Not in the mood for tall tales, Rachel took Maia by the hand and walked back to the entrance of the school so that she could return the doll to the teacher. She was halfway there when Monique, a living replica of the doll Rachel was carrying, except for the tail, of course, approached her with her matching daughter, Abigail.

'Rachel!' Monique stepped forward to kiss her on the cheek, a greeting that was awkwardly returned by Rachel. 'It's so good to see you again.'

'Hello, Monique,' said Rachel. She held the doll up. 'Does this belong to Abigail? It seems that Maia thinks she gave it to her.'

'That's because she did,' Monique said as she smiled and looked down at Abigail proudly. 'She has so many Barbies and when Maia told her she didn't even have one, she said she wanted to give her one of hers. We're trying to teach the children about generosity, so it looks like it's working.' She gave a small laugh.

Then, before Rachel had a chance to respond, Monique reached into her handbag and pulled out a brightly coloured piece of paper with Maia's name written on it in glitter glue.

'This is an invite to Abigail's birthday party next week,' Monique said as she passed it to Rachel. 'We're really hoping Maia can make it.'

'It's a *Frozen* party!' Maia explained, her eyes shining with excitement. She grabbed the invitation from her mother's hand before Rachel could ask what a frozen party was, although she did have a vague idea. A strange obsession with all things wintry seemed to have swept the nation since the release of the animated film and now every little girl wanted to have a dress-up party in honour of the movie. Added to this was the incessant singing of the theme song which, while it had started off as something cute, had grown into an unbearable cacophony of little girls' voices. Maia hadn't been immune.

Rachel looked down at her daughter, who couldn't seem to keep still, and then back up at Monique. She was amazed at how much her daughter's personality changed when she was around the children from school. Where usually she was obedient and pleasant, she transformed into a needy, whiny little girl who threw tantrums when she didn't get her way.

'It's at Papachinos,' Monique said, 'that child-friendly place in Bryanston? Have you been there?'

'Not yet,' Rachel replied. 'I've heard it's great, though.'

'I'm just glad that we don't have to sit in a Spur or a Mike's Kitchen any more. Remember how those used to be the only places you could go if you had kids and wanted to go out for a meal?' Monique rolled her eyes.

Rachel smiled and nodded, placing her hand firmly on Maia's shoulder.

'We will definitely try our best to be there,' she said.

'We've also got someone to look after the children so that us moms can have a bit of a party as well,' Monique added with a wink.

'Thank you,' Rachel said. 'We've got to go now but I'll let you know by the end of the week.'

Monique spotted another mom to deliver an invitation to and, grabbing Abigail by the hand, she darted off, calling out a greeting as she went. Rachel handed the doll back to Maia. She wondered whether she should talk to her about her views on accepting gifts from her friends at school but decided it could wait for another time.

Instead she took Maia's backpack from her and the two of them began their slow walk home through the quiet suburban streets filled with the lazy buzz of cicadas. The occasional car drove past them but, for the most part, the streets belonged to them that day.

'Abigail had her birthday circle today,' Maia said, barely looking up as she stroked the hair of her new Barbie, 'and her mommy brought blue *Frozen* cupcakes for the whole class.'

'That's nice, my girl.'

'Can you bring cupcakes for my birthday circle?'

'I'm sure I can,' Rachel replied, too tired to give Maia a response that would inspire an argument.

'*Blue* ones?'

Rachel smiled and nodded, switching the backpack to her other hand.

Maia squealed in excitement. 'Wait, Mama,' she said, holding the doll up for Rachel to take. Then she pulled off her jersey and, her face solemn in concentration, placed the neck of it around the crown of her head. Rachel waited and watched, trying to work out what Maia was doing. When she had finished her adjustments, Maia brushed the jersey out and looked up at Rachel with a big smile on her face.

'Look, Mama!' she said triumphantly. 'Long hair like a princess!'

Rachel couldn't hold back her smile and she laughed out loud as Maia flicked her 'hair' around, combing the folds of cloth with her small brown fingers as though they were strands of hair. Maia laughed, too, as she ran around her mother, singing the theme song from *Frozen* in her sweet high voice.

'Come, you silly thing,' Rachel said finally, taking Maia by the hand. 'You may be a princess but this maid needs to get back to work.'

chapter 5

CHRIS GRABBED A banana from the fruit bowl and his keys from the kitchen counter, the clock telling him that he was already late for work. He looked around to see if he was missing anything important and, satisfied that he wasn't, hurried out to his car.

Today was the first day of Michelle's 'rest' and he had left her to sleep in, being as quiet as he could while he showered and got dressed so that he didn't wake her. He walked up the driveway, his work shoes clicking on the cold slate which this morning was covered in a thin layer of frost and leaves. When he was a child one of his chores in autumn had been to sweep the dead leaves into piles and put them into black trashbags. Now he had Richmond to do that, and to make sure that everything else in the garden was in order.

He had almost reached the car when he saw Rachel walking towards the house. She was wearing a thick woollen jersey over her blue and white uniform and had her arms folded tightly around her chest from the cold. Chris wasn't a fan of maids in uniforms but, as it turned out, Rachel had told them that she preferred working in a uniform because it kept her normal clothes from getting dirty. So Chris had had to learn to accept its presence in the house, even though it was a constant reminder to him that he'd become a person who employed a servant.

Rachel hadn't seen him yet. She rubbed her arms in an attempt to get the blood circulating. Even though Chris knew her light went off at 20:30 every night, he thought she looked tired. He couldn't imagine what she was going through. He still found it difficult to engage with her about anything other than what he and Michelle needed her to do for them in the house.

'Rachel!' Chris called out and she looked up, startled at the sound of his voice. 'I'm glad I bumped into you. How are you doing?'

'I'm well, Mr Jordaan,' Rachel replied.

Rachel's return to formality baffled Chris and made him deeply uncomfortable, but he didn't know whether to say something about it or not. 'I just wanted to tell you that Michelle will be at home today.'

'Okay. Is she sick?'

'No. The doctor just said that she needed to rest a lot more for the baby so we've decided that she'll stop working and stay at home for the next few months.'

Chris watched Rachel process the information but her face was emotionless, betraying nothing of what she might be feeling or thinking. He and Michelle never talked about the baby when Rachel was within hearing, unless it was absolutely necessary. Now was one of those times.

'I just thought I'd let you know,' Chris concluded.

Rachel nodded. 'I'll make sure I don't disturb her,' she said.

Chris didn't know how to respond to this. Rachel had misunderstood him. His reason for telling her about Michelle staying home was not to make her feel like an intruder but more to let her know why Michelle would be there so much from now on.

'That won't be a problem,' he said, looking at the time on his iPhone and realising that he was even later than he thought. 'Sorry – I've got to get out of here.'

Chris climbed into his car, simultaneously starting the engine and pushing the button to open the electric gate. While he waited for it to open, he looked in the rear view mirror and saw Rachel standing at the entrance, waiting for him to leave before she went inside to start her work for the day. Her small, still figure, so upright and alone, cut deep into his heart. He rolled down the driver's side window.

'Do you need me to get you anything from the shops on the way home?'

Rachel shook her head. 'No, thank you. I'll be okay.'

'Okay, then,' Chris said, wanting to say more but not knowing what.

He reversed out of the driveway and, as he waited for the electric gate to close, saw Rachel slip inside and close the front door.

Michelle was right. This was going to be unbearable. He turned his music on and joined the other cars on their way to work.

Michelle lay in bed, the closed door to the bedroom separating her from the rest of the house. She heard the front door open and Rachel come in, followed by Hugo's excited barking as he greeted her.

Ignoring a wave of nausea, Michelle got up and walked to the door. She reached out a hand to open it, but just before her fingers touched the handle she froze. The voice was there again, whispering, accusing, saying her name. It was always present somewhere in her head. Her hand started shaking and she pulled it back. She couldn't do it. She couldn't face Rachel. She slid down the wall until she was sitting on the floor with her back against the door.

It wasn't your fault. It could have happened to anyone.

These were words Chris had said to her constantly and, as much as she tried to force herself to believe them and to repeat them to herself, she was unable to do so.

There was one simple reason.

It *was* her fault.

She knew it.

Chris knew it.

And, worst of all, Rachel knew it.

Rachel walked quietly down the passage that led to the Jordaans' bedroom, trying to work out where in the house Michelle was. The door was closed. She stopped outside it and listened, but all she heard was the sound of her own breathing. Perhaps Michelle was still asleep, even though by now it was past lunchtime. The Audi was still in the driveway. She went back down the passage to the kitchen, where she set up the ironing board and turned on the iron. She had been planning to vacuum this afternoon but now that it seemed Michelle was still here and possibly resting, it looked like she would have to save the noisy work for tomorrow.

Since Michelle had been staying at home, the atmosphere between them had been very difficult. Michelle barely acknowledged that Rachel was there at all. If they had exchanged more than a few sentences, it was a lot, and these were only really when Michelle told her she was going out. It was very confusing. If anything, Rachel should be the one ignoring Michelle but here she found herself being treated as though *she* had done something unforgiveable, as if she were at fault.

She picked up one of Michelle's cotton shirts from the laundry pile and laid it on the ironing board, flattening out the soft material before placing the hot iron on it, making the wrinkles disappear stroke by steady stroke. When she was satisfied she hung the shirt on a wooden hanger. Next she picked up a pair of blue jeans. She tried to work a wrinkle out, but the stubborn crease refused to be smoothed. She pushed down harder, moving the hot iron back and forth roughly. Suddenly she felt a stinging sensation on her forearm. She pulled back in pain. She had burned herself on the edge of the iron. As she watched, she saw a dark line form on her skin. She quickly walked over to the sink and turned on the cold tap, holding her arm under the flow of the water while she waited for the pain to subside. She felt tears coming and bit down hard on her lip. Her mind went back to Michelle. Rachel was the one who had been wronged and yet here she was cleaning up after the woman. She was the one who needed money to support her family, yet Michelle and Chris had more money than they knew what to do with. She was the one who had –

Yet Michelle was the one who was about to have a baby.

Rachel turned off the water and patted her arm dry on a piece of kitchen towel. She debated whether to apply some ointment on the burn from the emergency kit in the cupboard in the passage, but opted not to. She returned to the ironing board and waited for the steam to hiss.

Chris leaned over his drawing board and his latest project. He wanted to finish proofing the document one more time before it was sent out to the client, and he hoped to get it done before lunch. The office was a quiet hum of activity, all of his colleagues submerged in their own work. Suddenly the door burst open and Hannes rushed into the room, his glasses almost falling from his nose. He came to a skidding halt beside Chris.

'Sorry, man! I thought you were still out with a client.'

'I just got back,' Chris told him. 'What are you looking for?'

'The plans for Southbridge Mall.'

'In the cupboard,' Chris said amiably. He turned his attention back to the plans in front of him.

If ever there was someone from the office Chris would consider a friend, it was this short, stocky man. He and Hannes had started at the firm around the same time and had ended up working on the same projects as the years passed. Where Chris was married, Hannes was awkwardly single, the kind of guy who tried his best to change the situation but ended up digging the hole deeper with every attempt he made at dating.

Chris listened to Hannes rummaging through the cupboard, find the plans he was looking for and close the door with a crash. Instead of leaving right away, though, he came and stood on the other side of the table where he waited for Chris to look up at him.

'What's wrong?'

'Nothing,' Hannes said, fumbling with the plans. 'I just wanted to ask how things were at home.'

Chris smiled vaguely. 'Everything's good,' he said.

'And Michelle?'

'Um … she's okay, thanks. Has her ups and downs.' Chris began to realise that escaping this uninvited heart to heart wasn't going to be easy.

'I can imagine,' Hannes said, shaking his head.

'What do you mean?'

'*Ag*, just that, you know, it's a sad story.'

'What? Michelle staying at home is a sad story?' Chris was not going to play this game.

Hannes persevered nevertheless. 'No, um, you know. The whole thing with the maid,' he said.

Chris shook his head and looked away. He was irritated that his personal issues were being brought up at work, even if it was Hannes; it was the one place he was always able to keep things in control.

'It was an accident, Hannes,' he said shortly.

Before Hannes had a chance to comment both men were distracted by a tap at the door. Glossy red hair complementing an emerald green blouse and a wide friendly smile caused them both instantly to forget what they had been saying.

'I'm popping out to the mall,' said Anja. 'Can I get you guys anything?'

'I'll come with you,' Chris said impulsively. He'd had no intention of going out at lunch today but the conversation with Hannes had left him in need of some fresh air.

'Cool,' Anja said. 'Shall we go in your car?'

Chris nodded and picked up his jacket. Hannes stood sheepishly to one side, making no move to tag along. Where his tact was lacking, his discernment still functioned, Chris thought with something like grim satisfaction.

'Let's go, Anja,' he said.

'I'm finished,' Rachel called out, her voice echoing through the house.

She waited a few moments to see if Michelle would respond and, hearing nothing, she opened the front door and let herself out. As she entered her room she was overcome by a wave of tiredness. She flopped down on her bed, her arms by her sides.

Over the past few weeks the fires of resentment had died down but they had left something behind, she'd discovered: a seed of bitterness that was lodged in her heart. It was a physical presence. She could feel it, like an alien thing, sitting right beside the pain of her loss. Resentment first, then bitterness. Both emotions were growing inside her like a poisonous plant, their roots intertwining as they flourished and got stronger. She wasn't a malicious person by nature but as she felt this new emotion flowing through her veins, Rachel could feel it changing her. Now she lay on her bed without moving and allowed herself to surrender to it. Eyes closed, helpless in its surge, she submitted as wave upon wave of hatred moved relentlessly through her.

Michelle had been sitting on her bed when she heard Rachel call out. She closed her laptop and contemplated answering her, but as she sat in silence, she knew she couldn't allow this to be her first interaction with Rachel. She listened as the front door opened and then closed and waited until she heard Rachel's footsteps fading up the driveway before she stood up.

Her phone buzzed as a message came through. She picked it up and glanced at the screen. The message was from Karlien, her closest friend. Karlien had been trying to get hold of her all day but Michelle had ignored the calls. Right now her desire to spend time with any of her friends was low.

Been calling you all day! We're going to movies tonight – let me know if you're coming. #chickflick

Michelle sighed and typed in a reply.

Not feeling great hey. Maybe next time.

She waited for Karlien to text back. The house was quiet now that Rachel was gone, not even Hugo snuffling at the door. Rachel must have left him outside in the garden.

Just promise you won't become one of those pregnant women who never leaves the house.

I'll try :)

Get better.

Michelle slipped the phone into her pocket and opened the bedroom door. She padded down the passage through the quiet house and into the kitchen. Her shopping from a few days ago was still in its packaging on the counter. A vase and some ceramics for the house. She began to unwrap them, carefully peeling away the plastic coverings. She placed the vase on the big polished table in the living room and the three ceramic hearts on the mantelpiece above the fireplace. She took a few paces back, narrowed her eyes at the arrangement, then stepped forward and adjusted one of the hearts slightly so that the spacing between each was exactly even. The room was cold. It might be a good idea to make a fire this evening, the first one of autumn. She bent down and took some wood from the basket beside the fireplace and began to stack it in the grate.

As she lit a match and held it to one of the logs, Michelle knew she was going to have to interact with Rachel sooner or later. Tomorrow. She would do it tomorrow. She blew softly on the small flickers of flame and watched them grow, the yellow heat beginning to consume the wood. She heard the front door open and stood up just as Chris came into the room. He came straight over to her and took her in his arms. She kissed him on the cheek.

'Hey, you,' Chris said, holding her tightly.

'Hey.'

'This is nice,' he said, motioning towards the fire.

'I thought we should use it tonight. It's cold.'

Chris took off his jacket and sat down on the couch, kicking his shoes off and putting his socked feet on the coffee table.

'And, apart from this, what did you get up to today?' he asked, smiling.

'Not much,' Michelle replied. 'Stuck around here and worked. Dealt with some emails.'

Satisfied with her handiwork, Michelle sat down beside her husband on the couch and rested her head on his shoulder. The warm light from the fire reflected on their faces as the flames licked lazily at the wood.

'You speak to Rachel?'

Michelle sat up, taking her time as she thought about how best to answer him.

'No.'

'Why not?'

'We were on separate sides of the house, so I didn't really get a chance.'

Michelle could tell that her excuse rang false because not even she believed it. She felt Chris shift his weight on the couch. He put his arm around her and pulled her back towards him.

'You can't avoid her forever,' he said gently.

'I know.'

They sat in silence, watching the flames dance around each other in rhythmic steps only they knew the moves to. Michelle reflected that it had been a while since the two of them had just sat in silence next to each other and the warmth of Chris's body was comforting.

Silence between couples was one of the things they disagreed on. Chris had always said that one of his nightmares would be if they ended up like those older couples you saw in restaurants who went an entire meal without talking to each other, each staring ahead and eating their food in silence. In his opinion, this was a sign that your relationship had died and that you had nothing left to talk about. Although Michelle partly agreed with him, she also took another view; she looked at those silent couples and saw something different. In her mind, the ability to be quiet with someone was a sign that you were truly comfortable with that person, that you no longer needed to talk to communicate. The ability to be silent meant that you knew each other inside out and were content simply to sit peacefully in each other's presence.

As they sat together now and stared into the fire, she knew that this silence fell into the latter category. Chris knew what she was struggling with and she knew that he knew. They didn't need to talk about it.

Chris scrolled through his Facebook profile as the fire died down. Michelle was taking a bath, the remains of their takeaway dinner on the coffee table beside his feet. He decided it was time to change his profile picture and clicked through his photo album to find something he liked. A friend's wedding he and Michelle had attended a couple of months ago had a few decent ones but nothing looked quite right. He opened up the album from the Run Jozi marathon he'd completed last October. There was a photo of him crossing the finishing line, his body a few kilograms lighter than it was right now and looking good in his running gear. He hit upload and, after aligning the thumbnail, set it as his profile picture.

He was about to turn the tablet off when he heard a beep and saw the red notification telling him that the photo had been liked. By Anja. The digital approval brought a smile to his face. Then the app beeped again and he saw that she had written a comment on the photo.

A man of many talents! #superboss

Chris couldn't think of anything smart to say in reply (and technically he wasn't her boss) so he made his way to her photographs instead, starting what had become a nightly ritual for him of going through Anja's past adventures. He chuckled to himself as he read some of the exchanges she'd had with her friends. Anja had a great sense of humour, sharp and funny. She was good company.

Before signing out he went back to her comment and liked it. It would be telling her he had received her message, but wouldn't be misconstrued or look inappropriate to anyone else who might be interacting with her.

chapter 6

RACHEL SAT ON the bed beside her daughter and tucked the blue blanket around the little girl's body. Maia lay on her back with her Barbie doll in her hands, whispering secrets into her ear. It made Rachel smile. She had hardly put the doll down since they'd got home.

'Are you ready to sleep?' she asked.

Maia nodded but didn't look up. She began to stroke the doll's long golden hair.

'What are you thinking, little one?' Rachel prompted.

'Why is my hair not long like Barbie's or Abigail's?' Maia asked.

'Because our hair doesn't grow like white people's,' Rachel replied, bending and planting a kiss on her daughter's head.

'But Beyoncé isn't white and her hair is long,' Maia pointed out logically.

'That's not her real hair,' Rachel told her.

'Don't lie, Mama.'

'I'm not lying,' Rachel replied, trying to hold back her laughter. 'She buys her hair from a shop and they sew it into her real hair.'

'Oh.' Maia looked up at her mother with interest. 'Where does the shop get the hair from?'

'Some of the hair is made from plastic but, if you have money like Beyoncé, you get it from Indian women. They cut their hair off and sell it to the shop.'

Rachel watched Maia process the information and tried to hide her amusement. She had an inkling of what was going through Maia's head. While she was growing up in Inhassoro, white people in the village were rare, but she had a distinct memory of once seeing some German tourists at the market, and she especially remembered being fascinated by the women's hair – long strands the colour of beach sand that went right down their backs and moved and floated as they walked around shopping for souvenirs. Rachel had watched in amazement and afterwards dedicated weeks of prayers to Jesus in the hope that he would give her hair just like those women's.

'Mama,' Maia said, 'can I ask you something?'

'What?' Rachel said.

'Can you get me some Indian hair from – '

'Okay, girl, it's time for you to go to sleep now.'

'One more question, Mama.'

'Quickly.'

'When are you going to teach me to swim?'

Rachel looked down at her daughter and stroked her forehead, the hope in Maia's eyes bringing a wave of warmth through her soul. She couldn't believe how fast she was growing up.

'Not yet, Maia, but soon.'

'And then can I swim in the ocean when we go visit Mozambique?'

'Yes. Time for sleep now,' Rachel said. She leaned forward and kissed her. 'Sleep dreams, my little girl.'

Maia gave a big contented sigh. Carefully, she tucked her mermaid Barbie doll beneath the blue blanket beside her, arranging the golden hair on the pillow. Then she closed her eyes and Rachel turned off the harsh overhead light. She left the bedside lamp on.

As Maia's breathing deepened, Rachel knelt on the floor next to the bed and reached under it. She pulled out a red biscuit tin, which she took across to the table. Quietly she prised off the lid and sifted through the contents until she found her passport. She flipped through the pages to the latest stamp. The date showed that her visa would expire in just a few weeks' time. She would need to go to Home Affairs soon to get it renewed, a process that usually proved to be both humiliating and time consuming. She always dreaded going there.

Most of the guards outside the building carried sjamboks, large plastic whips that they swung back and forth to herd the foreign nationals in and out of the premises. No one dared complain. They were all well aware that any protest would be detrimental to the renewal of their visas. Some of the guards would stop people from entering and only allow them access to the building once they had paid a bribe. All power rested in their hands and everyone knew it.

Fortunately for her, Rachel was familiar with the process and not as intimated as she used to be when she'd first arrived in South Africa. Now she knew exactly where to go and how the system worked. Usually, she found herself standing in a line with about 50 other immigrants all waiting for their applications to be processed by an officer who would take frequent bathroom breaks and personal phone calls. On good days the process would take about three hours, although this was never a certainty, and by the end of it she would emerge with another six months of security. She dreamed of the day, not too far off now, when she would be able to fill out an application form for permanent residence.

She put the passport back in the biscuit tin but before she closed it her eye lit on the cowry shell she had picked up on the beach at Inhassoro the day she had left Mozambique. She took it out. The enamel shone in the light of the lamp but somehow, like Rachel herself, she thought wryly, the shell had lost its vibrancy over time. Perhaps it was the absence of the warm waters of the Indian Ocean that had taken its toll on both of their bodies. But still the shell reminded her of home. She brought it to her lips and blew gently into its underside until a low hum resonated through the room. Instead of returning it to the tin, she placed it on the table, deciding she would give it to Maia in the morning. It would be something that would tell her where she came from. It might not be an expensive doll or an elaborate birthday party, but it was something precious. Something from home, a part of who she was.

Rachel slid the tin back beneath the bed, then turned on the TV with the volume down low. She cleared everything off the table and spread a threadbare blanket over its surface. Then she turned her attention to her own pile of ironing, starting with her blue and white uniform for the following day.

Michelle sat on the toilet seat, waiting for the pregnancy test to give her an answer. They had done everything by the book: from the timing that they had sex to the food she had eaten and not eaten that month. She had even lain with her pelvis in the air for an hour after they had had sex in the hope that the angle would encourage Chris's sperm in their important mission.

This wasn't the first time she had held one of these tests in her hand but this time, as with the ones before, she was hoping it would be the last. The negatives had happened too often for her not to be worried but she still held onto the belief that this time it would be different.

When they had first started trying to conceive, she had let Chris know whenever she was about to take a test but now, four years and three miscarriages in, it was something that she did privately. Chris would always get too excited in the build-up and when the answer came out negative he would be unable to hide his disappointment. This, in turn, would lead to a difficult week, of insecurity from her side and compensation from his as they tried to deal with their failure. By keeping it to herself, she reasoned, she made things easier, and while it meant that she went through the journey alone each time, it also meant that she dealt with the disappointment faster.

With Chris at work and Rachel at the shops with Maia, she had the house to herself. She stared at the small window, willing the right sign to appear. The colours on the stick began to change and she watched as one line emerged from the beige background. She waited a little longer until she was certain and then she tossed the stick into the bathroom trashcan.

Unbidden, the tears came and she stayed where she was, sitting on the toilet seat. Her heart felt like it was being squeezed by a fist in her chest and she felt the beginnings of a headache. Perhaps it was time to consider the reality that she and Chris might not be able to have children. The thought was unbearable. She tried to stop herself from crying but then, realising that she was completely alone in house and that no one could see or hear her, she just let go. She put her face in her hands and sobbed. She cried until her insides hurt.

When it seemed she was spent, she stood up and looked at her reflection in the bathroom mirror. She was a pitiful sight – smeared make-up and puffy red eyes. Get a grip, Michelle, she told herself. She turned on the faucet and splashed her face with cold water. She reached down, took the pregnancy test stick out of the trashcan, wrapped it in toilet paper and took it downstairs to put in the bin outside the kitchen door. No point in Chris coming across it inadvertently.

Rachel and Maia walked through Checkers Hypermarket, Maia's tiny hand in Rachel's as they navigated their way through the crowded aisles of food and products towards the Money Market counter at the back of the store. The Money Market was a cash-send facility the department store offered, which allowed customers to deposit in South African rands and send the money to family in the currency of the country they came from. This was how she sent money back to her parents in Mozambique, which she did once a month on the day the Jordaans paid her.

They joined the back of the line that snaked towards the counter. Rachel checked her old Nokia to see if she had any messages. Her mother would often send her an sms to let her know that she was at the cash depot in Inhassoro so that if there was a problem with the transaction, Rachel could sort it out right away. There was no message today. She put a fingertip into the envelope she had in her hand and counted the rands inside once more just to make sure that she had the correct amount.

Maia had brought the Barbie doll along for the journey which served Rachel just fine because it meant she wouldn't have to keep the child entertained while she shopped. Things moved much more slowly when Maia was with her so she appreciated anything that made the task easier.

The cashier at the Money Market stand indicated to Rachel to step forward. Rachel did so, and placed the envelope and her passport on the counter.

'Where to?' the assistant asked. Her plastic braids were held together by a bright purple band.

'Inhassoro, Mozambique.'

The woman slid a piece of paper and a pen across the counter and started talking to one of the other assistants, who was leaning against the counter with an earphone in her one ear listening to music on her cellphone.

Rachel was just beginning to fill out the form when she felt a tug on her sleeve.

'Wait, Maia,' she said without looking down. 'Don't do that.' She went back to the form. When she was halfway through she heard a familiar high piping voice coming from about a metre away. Clear as a bell, she heard her daughter say: 'Can I have your hair?'

She whipped around. Maia was standing in front of an Indian woman, who looked to be in her thirties. Her hands were behind her back, Mermaid Barbie clutched tightly in one of them, and her chin was pointed upwards as she looked earnestly into the complete stranger's face. The Indian woman stared down at the little girl, obviously uncomprehending, which only prompted Maia to repeat her question, louder this time so as to make sure it was understood.

Rachel stopped writing and hurried over, her cheeks burning. She grasped Maia by the arm, muttering apologies to the woman, who didn't seem to see any humour in the moment. She picked Maia up and sat her on the counter. When Maia opened her mouth to speak she silenced her with a fierce look that told her she had better stay right there and not go wandering off and accost any other likely looking candidates. Rachel hastily finished the form, picked Maia off the counter and set her firmly on the floor.

'Maia,' she said, kneeling down so that she was on her level. 'Do not do that again. It is not good manners to ask ladies for their hair. Do you understand?'

'But you said ...' Maia knew she was taking a chance but was standing her ground.

'Stop now,' Rachel said.

Maia knew that tone. She whispered something in her Barbie's plastic ear but said no more about it.

Chris sat at his desk, staring blankly at the screen of his desktop. He was supposed to be working on a proposal for a new development but the 3pm slump had hit and he was struggling to stay focused.

He let his eyes roam around the open plan office and saw the rest of his co-workers working at their stations, the air filled with the quiet patter of fingers on keyboards. He watched Anja Fouche exit from her boss's office across the way and make her way to her desk.

She was oblivious to his scrutiny. She sat down and began to shuffle through the papers she'd been carrying, chewing on her bottom lip in concentration as she tried to create order.

His phone buzzed and he looked down to see that he had a message from Michelle. She was feeling sick and didn't feel like going to movies as they'd planned. Chris texted back, asking if he could get her anything, to which she replied that she just wanted to sleep. He was free to go out and do whatever he wanted that evening.

Chris contemplated staying at home to keep Michelle company but decided to take her up on her offer of a night off. He opened a new email and typed Hannes's address into it, sending him a quick message even though his friend was sitting on the other side of the office.

Movies tonight?

Chris hit send and sat back, looking across the office as he waited for Hannes's reply. Instead his friend's head suddenly appeared through the work station dividers. Hannes grinned and gave Chris a thumbs up.

Maria and Tapiwa were laughing so hard that drivers stuck in traffic turned to see what the commotion was on the street corner.

'What did the woman *say*?' Maria spluttered. Her laughing turned into a wheezing cough and she tried to bring it under control.

'Nothing,' Rachel said as she caught her breath. She had found herself laughing just as hard as her friends as she told the story of the incident with Maia at the Money Market counter in Checkers. 'She just changed lines and refused to look at us.'

'Poor thing,' Tapiwa chuckled, her shoulders still shaking with mirth.

The laughter started to fade and brief silence descended. The three friends hadn't met together on the grass for a while and there was a lot to catch up on. Maria had brought a packet of crisps along and a few moments of steady crunching covered the quiet before the next topic.

'I have to renew my visa on Monday,' Rachel said, wiping her greasy fingers on the grass.

'Make sure you have your letter of employment,' Tapiwa said.

'Yes. That paper is like gold,' Maria added.

'Are you sleeping there on Sunday night?' Tapiwa asked. 'At Home Affairs?'

'No, I can't sleep on the streets with Maia. And anyway I'm going to ask the Jordaans if I can leave her here while I go.'

Maria and Tapiwa exchanged a look. Rachel shook her head, knowing what they were thinking. It was a little presumptuous of her to expect her employers to allow her child to stay unattended on the property but she believed they had a strong enough relationship to allow her do this. Chris and Michelle would both be at work so she knew that asking was more of a formality than an imposition and Maia would stay in her room.

'Are you paying someone to stand in line for you?' Maria asked.

Rachel nodded.

'How much?'

'Too much.'

chapter 7

RACHEL WALKED DOWN the cold driveway from her room to the Jordaans' house. Her feet ached. The leaves that Richmond had cleared had been replaced by a fresh batch from the oak tree this morning. The Audi parked outside the front door, with a thin layer of frost on its windscreen, told her that Michelle was still in the house. She took a deep breath. What was waiting for her on the other side of the front door today, she wondered. Would Michelle stay closed up in her room or would she actually have the decency to acknowledge her presence?

She walked into the warm house, opening curtains and windows as she made her way to the kitchen. A glance down the passage showed her that the bedroom door was firmly closed, as it had been the day before. Michelle was probably still in bed. It was early, after all.

She froze the moment she saw Michelle sitting at the kitchen table, the steam from two mugs of tea curling through the cold air in front of her.

'I made you some tea,' Michelle said awkwardly, standing up.

Still rooted to the spot, Rachel watched Michelle approach her, mug extended like a peace offering. Rachel took it from her, barely registering the heat burning her hand as she gripped it tightly.

'Thank you.'

The words hung in the air as the two women took each other in properly for the first time since their uncomfortable session the Sunday evening before Rachel returned to work. Michelle looked the way that Rachel felt inside: tired and sad. Michelle opened her mouth to say something, the words struggling to surface.

'Rachel …'

Rachel waited for Michelle to continue, trying to suppress the hot fire deep inside her, its flames sparking and licking at her like tongues. She stood perfectly still, knowing that her face betrayed nothing of what she was feeling. She could see that Michelle was disconcerted by her posture and did not know how to read her. She wanted to scream, to run over to Michelle and grab her by the shoulders, shake her until her teeth rattled, take that hot mug of tea and throw it in her face like acid. But she stood, waiting.

'I … I'm going to be working in the study today,' Michelle said. 'Just in case you – Just in case you need anything.'

Rachel nodded. Waited.

Michelle edged past her. Still Rachel did not move. She did not watch Michelle leave the kitchen. She did not hear her footsteps in the passage.

When she was gone Rachel walked stiffly over to the sink. The mug was warm against her cold hands. She poured the tea down the drain in a slow brown stream. Then she turned on the hot water and began to rinse the dirty dishes.

Back in the bedroom with the door closed, Michelle found she was trembling. That had not gone well at all. She lay down on the bed and hugged a pillow to her stomach. She must have drifted off because when she woke with a start and sat up, feeling dizzy and nauseous, it was 9 am.

Realising with alarm that she was going to be sick, she bolted for the bathroom and slammed the door closed behind her. She lunged for the toilet, grateful for the first time ever that Chris had left the seat up, and vomited violently into the bowl, expelling from her stomach everything that she had eaten that morning and probably the night before.

Actually she had been feeling ill since she woke up that morning but the conversation – if she could even call it that – with Rachel seemed to have triggered a bout of morning sickness such as she hadn't experienced so far. Dr Pieterse had been telling her she was lucky: most of her patients reported horrible morning sickness. Other than not feeling herself over the last few weeks, Michelle hadn't actually been physically sick. Today was the first time that it seemed as though her body was turning on her. It had declared mutiny on her and all she could do was hold on as the storm raged inside of her.

She stood up shakily and wiped her lips with a wad of toilet paper. Leaning over the basin, she rinsed the bile and vomit from her mouth. She wiped the sweat that had formed on her forehead with her wrist and paused for a few seconds to see if she should expect another bout of nausea. Then she flushed the toilet.

As she looked down at her stomach a flash of resentment towards the baby moved through her, and she had a moment of yearning for her body to remain inhospitable and reject the pregnancy. She didn't deserve this child, not any more. Maybe order would be restored if it just wasn't there.

The emotion was immediately followed by a flood of guilt rushed through her. She splashed more cold water on her face in an attempt to clear her mind. Then she brushed her teeth vigorously and blew her nose.

In the study she sat at her desk staring out of the window and trying to think of what she would do to keep herself occupied today. She was finally coming to terms with the fact that she was not going to be able to keep herself as busy as she was accustomed to and although it still didn't sit well, she knew she had no option but to figure out a way to ease into this different routine.

She powered up her laptop and scanned through her emails. Then she opened her internet browser and typed a search request into Google: *what shouldn't I do when I'm pregnant?*

She waited as her request was considered by the web and watched as the front page of possible solutions filled the browser, with advice ranging from diet to activities. She scrolled through the advice with indifference, learning nothing new.

Rachel was standing in the flowerbed that ran along the exterior of the house cleaning the bathroom window when she heard the door open inside and then slam shut. This was followed by the unmistakable sound of Michelle vomiting – the second time today. Even through the thick pane of glass it made Rachel feel nauseous. She stopped wiping the glass and waited, listening to the muffled sounds of her employer's wretchedness. It took her right back to the early stages of her own pregnancy, with one moment in particular standing out. She had been standing in the line to get her passport stamped as she crossed from Mozambique into South Africa when the familiar nausea set in and, knowing that the customs official would not respond kindly to being vomited on by a traveller, she had used every bit of willpower she possessed to remain calm and keep everything inside. Once her passport had been stamped she ran to the bathrooms. Even though the facilities were blocked and covered in waste they could never have looked better to her than they did that day.

Rachel was brought back to the present by the sound of the toilet flushing and she waited until she was sure that Michelle had left the bathroom before she continued to clean the window. She wiped the pane until it squeaked before moving on to the next one. She found herself half smiling. There was a warm satisfaction in the thought of Michelle being in discomfort.

Michelle returned to her study. Her skin felt clammy and her mouth was dry from the vomiting. She had seen Rachel's shadow outside the bathroom window and had left the room feeling worse than when she had gone in. The idea of this child growing inside her under Rachel's watchful gaze, as she stood behind windows and in dark corners, silent, judging her, disturbed her terribly.

She typed another question into the search engine, each key that she hit laced with guilt: *abortion clinics johannesburg south africa.*

A list of facilities close to her location appeared in the browser. She swallowed hard and opened the first link. Hesitating only momentarily, she tapped the 'MORE INFO' section in the corner of the window and waited, her eyes not leaving the screen. At the prompt, her heart pounding in her ears, she entered her name and email address on the digital form.

Rachel fell back onto her bed and closed her eyes. The weight of the work that day had left her physically exhausted. It was very quiet in the room and the lack of noise was soothing and unsettling at the same time. Usually she spent her afternoons once she'd knocked off with Maia, either playing in the park down the road or preparing their evening meal. The extra time she now had on her hands brought her no rest but rather an awareness of how alone she was, the emptiness amplified by the stillness.

She had no appetite for food nor the energy to prepare any. Even though there was still an hour of daylight left, she pulled the blue blanket over her head and slipped into a deep sleep.

'How are you feeling?' Chris asked as he and Michelle strolled down the quiet street, the last rays of sun filtering through the autumn leaves. It had been his idea that they take Hugo for a walk every day when he got home from work and, thanks to their scarves and jackets, it was turning out to be a pleasant activity. Most of the traffic had died down by this time and they joined the other dog walkers and occasional jogger as they made their way along the neighbourhood's quiet avenues, peering into other people's properties, the ones that weren't incarcerated behind forbidding walls, and giving their opinions on their design and upkeep. The cold air burned their nostrils while the smell of the autumn fires added a distinct flavour that signified the start of winter.

'Like my body is making a human,' Michelle said.

Chris smiled, but Michelle wasn't looking at him. Brown and golden leaves crunched beneath their feet. Hugo ran as far as his leash would allow, jerking at Chris's arm as he charged ahead between sniffing at trees and street poles.

'You get any sleep today?'

'I tried. The problem is that if I sleep too much in the day I'm up all night.'

'I like what they've done with the entrance here,' Chris said, stopping beside a house where a new security wall and gate had recently been installed. The high walls were clad in sandstone. 'We should think about doing something like that around the fireplace one day,' he added. Michelle nodded.

They greeted a young man in a vest and shorts who was jogging past them, his warm breath silver against the cold air. They both shivered and, huddling closer together, carried on walking in silence. Chris linked Michelle's arm in his. He was trying to figure out if this was the best time to ask Michelle the question that was uppermost in his mind but he didn't want to ruin this moment of intimacy, contentment even.

'We spoke,' Michelle said.

Chris looked at her, but her eyes were on the ground ahead.

'And?'

'It was awkward. But we spoke.'

Chris stopped walking and made Michelle do the same. He took his wife's face in his hands so that she was looking directly at him. Her eyes were watery but he couldn't tell whether this was from emotion or the cold.

'It will get easier as time goes by,' he said.

Michelle nodded. The defiant set of her chin at that moment made something catch in his throat. He kissed her softly on her mouth.

'I'm proud of you,' he said.

Rachel lay in the bathtub, the water shielding her body from the cold night air that drifted in through the window she had left open. Sometimes she enjoyed the contrast of temperatures, her cold face peeking through the steam that rose from the hot water. She slid down onto her back and submerged her head, the night sounds from the garden disappearing as the silence of the water took over. She could hear her heart beating in her ears and as she held her breath she found herself wishing that she could just dissolve into the water that surrounded her.

To disappear, to escape, to no longer be needed and to no longer care.

She felt trapped, caught between her pain and her obligations. The days moved so slowly. She no longer experienced the extremes of emotion she had gone through when Maia – now she just felt dead inside, her soul a dry husk that no water could revive. As her lungs ran out of oxygen, she resisted the urge to come up for air, allowing the pain in her chest to distract her from that other pain, the one that throbbed continually like a club to her heart.

Is this what it felt like, she thought to herself as her lungs contracted and her heart beat faster. *Maia? Is this what dying feels like?*

Blood roaring in her ears, she held herself down until the first drops of water began to slip through her mouth and into her lungs. She came up quickly, coughing and spluttering and choking on water and air.

And then Rachel began to sob, her tears mixing with water as they ran down her face into the tub.

chapter 8

'ARE YOU SURE there isn't a job at one of the hospitals?' Rachel's mother asked her.

The landline in the Jordaans' kitchen was much clearer than the pay phone by the taxi rank and, while she had felt uncomfortable at first when Chris told her she was free to use their telephone to call home, she had slowly grown accustomed to this perk. She had told her mother not to call her on the line, though, on the chance that Michelle or Chris might pick up, but to rather text her when she was available to talk. Then if the house was empty, Rachel would call her back and they would spend about 20 minutes exchanging stories and catching up. Today, with the Jordaans at their respective offices, Maia at nursery school and Richmond working at his other job in the neighbourhood, she was relaxed on the white leather couch next to the phone.

'There's nothing, Mama,' Rachel replied, slipping into Portuguese like her mother. She took a sip of tea from the mug she held in her free hand. 'They barely have work for the local nurses so there's little chance of me finding something. Plus, if I changed jobs then I'd need to find a new place to stay.'

'It's a pity, but – '

'How is Father doing?'

'Better. He can walk again.'

The line went silent for a minute. Inevitably, they always ended up talking about Inhassoro and the local people's ongoing struggles there. This time Rachel brought the subject up first.

'Is there food in the shops yet?' she asked.

'We ran out of maize last week. Fortunately, I had enough to last us but others went hungry. Mr da Silva says there'll be more next week if his shipment makes it through customs. I don't know what we would do without your money, child … others are dying because they don't have a – '

'That won't happen to you, Mama,' Rachel said, cutting her off before things became too emotional. 'I get paid on Wednesday and I will wire the money to you in the afternoon. You should get it – '

Rachel stopped talking at the sound of the dial tone. The connection to Inhassoro was faulty, even on good days, and it wasn't unusual to have her conversations with her mother cut short this way. She considered calling her back but decided not to today. She still had work to do.

Even though things in Inhassoro were getting better, they were still far from good. She recalled how, just after the cyclone had hit, she and her mother had competed with seagulls for the tiny crabs that would end up being the only food they were able to find during that time. All crops and livestock were destroyed and clean water was something that you had to collect in buckets when it rained.

Scores of villagers died of dysentery and other water-borne diseases and she had witnessed with horror as friends and family members had seemed to melt into their skeletons. She was watching a village die. She had spent her days trying to ease the pain of those who were suffering.

Help, ironically, had come from the sea, the very thing that had destroyed them. While on a trip to Vilanculos with her mother to try and find food, Rachel had been walking along the beach when she noticed a large boat sailing towards the broken harbour which had been built by the Portuguese before she was born. The boat navigated the rocks and sandbanks in the harbour and came to a stop. She saw a man, probably in his thirties, climb out and secure the boat. He approached her and, with the help of a translator, asked her if she could go and gather the men in the village. When she had asked him why, he told her that he had brought food and that he needed help taking it from the boat. The news seemed too good to be true but a glance over the man's shoulder into the vessel revealed large bags of maize wrapped in plastic, stacked one on top of another.

Rachel ran back to the village and did what she had been asked, returning with as many as 50 able-bodied men and a larger crowd of women and children who wanted to see if she had been bewitched or if she was telling the truth.

The men got to work and, after a day of heavy toil, the maize was on the beach and the boat was empty. Rachel had managed to find a fresh coconut which she cracked open and brought to the man, a simple token of thanks for the salvation he had brought to her people. He accepted the coconut and drank the sweet milk gratefully, thanking her afterwards in English. When she responded in English, he looked surprised and started to engage with her, asking her questions about her life and her family.

Rachel found the man easy to talk to. In turn she asked him who he was and where he was from. He told her his name was Peter and that he had come from South Africa because he believed that God had wanted him to bring food to the people affected by the cyclone. He had started an NGO called Joint Aid Management and his goal was to use JAM to bring food and clean water to people who did not have access to it. Before he could continue, the elders of the village arrived to thank the man for his help and Rachel had to stand aside with the rest of the women and children.

Rachel never saw the man Peter again but so strong was the impression he had made on her that she decided, in her heart, that if a white man all the way from South Africa could do something to help her people, she would try to do the same.

It was the day she decided to train as a nurse.

Rachel went through the house methodically, room by room, cleaning and straightening as she went. She noticed Michelle's expensive Louis Vuitton handbag on the dining room table. As she moved to straighten the centrepiece she saw that the bag was open and that Michelle had left her purse in it. Rachel paused. Her heart started to beat hot and fast, betraying her intention before she even had a chance to acknowledge it.

Even though she knew she was alone, she looked around anxiously for a couple of minutes, ears straining for any sound. Then, quickly, nervously, she dipped her hand into the bag and slowly extracted the purse, her fingers trembling. She unfastened the silver clasp and the purse popped open. She looked inside and saw a wad of R100 and R200 notes, crisp from the ATM. She didn't need to count the money to know that what Michelle carried in her purse as change was more than she had in her red biscuit tin after years of saving.

She stared down at the money. She reached in and slid out a purple R100 note. Carefully, she folded it in half and placed it inside her bra, before returning the purse to the handbag.

Michelle would never notice one note missing, of this Rachel was sure. And she would add it to the money she was sending back to her mother, so she would benefit nothing from it personally. Again she looked around, just to make sure that ... Then she left the room, bending down to pet Hugo as he bounded up to greet her.

chapter 9

MICHELLE SAT IN the examination chair while Dr Pieterse moved the transducer across her belly, the cool blue gel helping the instrument move over her skin. Dr Pieterse stared at the screen next to the bed, the grey image morphing with each stroke while the sound of the baby's heartbeat filled the air with its frantic rhythm.

Michelle was in her twentieth week of her pregnancy. Today Chris had come with her for the foetal anomaly scan. She had told him he didn't need to, but he knew this was one of the 'milestone' scans and had cleared his morning so that he could accompany her to the clinic. Though he would never say it, their previous encounters with Dr Pieterse had left him anxious for the health of their child and, while she would never say it, Michelle shared his fear.

She had done everything that had been asked of her.

She'd put her career on hold, slowed down her life and submitted to the reality that her only purpose for the next few months was to create an environment in herself which would help the baby grow. It had been difficult at first but, as the weeks had turned into months, she had grown accustomed to days filled with reading, afternoon naps and converting one of their guest rooms into a room for the baby.

As much as she was doing everything she'd been instructed to do and she wished the baby no harm, her emotions remained confused and often dark. Somewhere deep down she still harboured the small hope that she would wake up one morning and find that the pregnancy had terminated in the night. Although she had been unable to bring herself to respond to the email she'd received from the women's clinic, which had arrived in her inbox the day after she'd made the connection, this inability to follow through had not taken away the desire for things to go back to the way they were before she had fallen pregnant.

With every centimetre that the baby grew, her soul grew heavier.

Dr Pieterse was jotting down notes on a pad of paper while Chris gazed at the screen, mesmerised by the movements of his baby. Michelle was still feeling a little queasy, but it was nothing compared to the nausea she had endured a few weeks earlier.

'Are you ready to find out the sex?' Dr Pieterse asked when she'd finished writing.

'No,' Michelle said quickly. She was unnerved by the question. While she and Chris had spoken about this issue in passing, she had a feeling that they would arrive at different conclusions.

'We haven't really decided yet,' Chris added, trying to soften Michelle's abrupt reply. 'Actually, we thought you'd only be able to tell the sex at the next scan.'

'New technology,' Dr Pieterse told him. 'We're able to tell earlier and earlier these days.'

Michelle looked at Chris and, over a couple of seconds, their eyes had an entire argument. Michelle wished that, just for once, they could be on the same page when it came to a big decision, but it would seem this was not going to be that time.

'Tell you what,' Dr Pieterse said, sensing that they weren't going to reach a resolution during the examination. 'You talk it through and when you come to a decision, just give me a call if you want to know.'

Michelle and Chris smiled back at the doctor, both a little embarrassed at the situation and relieved by Dr Pieterse's suggestion. Michelle leaned back into the chair and Dr Pieterse picked up the transducer once more.

'What you will need to do now, though, is look away from the screen because it's going to be pretty obvious what the sex is when I find out what's hiding – or not hiding – between the baby's legs.'

The car ride home was a journey made in silence, a way of travel that was becoming all too familiar to Chris these days. Michelle sat in the seat next to him with her sunglasses on, staring out of the window as if she was a million miles away.

They pulled up at a traffic light and Chris watched a young black street beggar with an obviously false limp making his way through the hawkers and people handing out pamphlets, imploring each of the drivers in the queue to part with their loose change. Chris had been driving past this beggar for more than five years now. He'd given him a sweater (one he'd really loved) on a particularly cold morning during the first few months they'd interacted, but his illusions had been shattered the very next day when he saw the man walking out of the gas station bathroom free of any physical deformity, warmly robed (in Chris's sweater) and talking animatedly on a cellphone.

Begging was an art in Johannesburg, he'd decided, and only the best performers walked away with the money. There was the young Malawian guy on Malibongwe and Hans Schoeman who did three somersaults in front of the cars while the light was red and then walked from driver to driver to collect his fee. Then there was the overweight woman who sat in the shade of the trees on Republic while her four children stood at each point of the intersection, breathing in fumes and bringing back their earnings to their pimp. The Rastafarian at Leslie and Hornbill could be quite abusive. He would hold out a black plastic bag to collect the trash from your car and his attitude was one that almost convinced you he was begging out of choice, not necessity, and that you owed him. Chris was also pretty sure he sold weed too.

While he was not one to judge their motivations or question their circumstances, there was a group of beggars on President Fouche and Hawken who always made his skin crawl. They were a group of white men in their fifties, burnt brown from the sun, with unkempt beards, who carried with them an air of superiority that could only have come from minds moulded by apartheid. They were constantly berating the black street vendors who shared the traffic light with them and, when they weren't holding up cardboard signs that bore slogans like 'Down But Still Trying', they were mocking the wealthy black people who drove past them in their out-of-the-box cars. White people seemed to give to this group with ease; perhaps they saw a version of themselves staring back at them. The beggars would take their 'wages' and buy cheap liquor from the bottle-store down the road. He saw them go in and out all the time.

Now the familiar discomfort set in as he saw the beggar with the limp determinedly approaching his window, holding out his hands in the universal sign for seeking alms. Chris shook his head and stared ahead, knowing that if he made eye contact, the man would not stop pleading until the lights changed and he drove off feeling like a heartless bastard.

'Why don't you want to know?' Chris asked.

Michelle was still gazing listlessly out the window, her sunglasses hiding her eyes.

'I just don't.'

'But there has to be a reason,' Chris persisted. The beggar was at his window now, mouthing something and looking desolate.

'I told you I'm fine with you finding out, as long as you keep it to yourself.'

'Like that's going to work out,' Chris said, studiously looking at the traffic light, the pleading beggar on his right and his disappointed wife on his left. At least his window was closed, creating the illusion that there was a hint of distance between the two of them.

'Just let it go, Chris,' Michelle said. 'Please?'

Chris gripped the steering wheel, silently urging the light to turn green so that he could drive away from the man who was now beginning seriously to bug him. He gave a short, sarcastic laugh and inched the car forward.

'What's that for?' Michelle asked.

'Because you're being childish.'

'Why are you turning on me, Chris?'

'Turning on you? How is showing you when you're in the wrong tur – '

His sentence was cut off by a knock on his window and he jumped, startled. For some unfathomable reason the beggar seemed to think now was an appropriate moment for him to tap on Chris's window to get his attention. Now, while he was clearly having an argument with his wife.

'What the FUCK do you WANT?' he yelled.

The man's eyes widened as he realised he'd probably gone too far. Enraged, Chris hit the horn in frustration just as the light turned green. The car in front of him honked back in retaliation, thinking Chris was honking at him, and Chris held up his hand apologetically. He looked over at Michelle and immediately regretted his angry reaction. Michelle hated cursing and, while Chris was not offended by it, he didn't use swear words often because of this, especially not in front of her.

'I'm sorry,' he said, but Michelle didn't respond.

Chris exhaled deeply and turned up the volume on the sound system, welcoming the way that the radio managed to cover up the silence for the rest of the ride home. At their front gate Richmond was raking up the leaves that had fallen during the night. They both waved at him as they drove in, but the minute Chris switched the engine off, Michelle got out of the car and strode into the house.

Chris could tell that the rest of the day was going to be a frosty one. He sat back, giving Michelle some time to reach the front door without him. As he gathered his things and climbed out of the car, he saw Rachel taking down her personal washing from the line outside her quarters. He waved at her but she didn't wave back. Perhaps she hadn't seen him. He activated the car alarm and walked heavily down the driveway to the house.

He could hear that Michelle was in the baby's room but he didn't follow her. Instead he went to the kitchen, where he took a bottle of water from the fridge and walked over to the breakfast nook, undoing his tie as he went. He stared out into the wintry garden, taking in Richmond's handiwork in the afternoon light.

The pool was still green.

Chris frowned, took a swig of water and went outside. He could smell the chlorine Richmond had put in but it didn't seem to be working. He walked slowly all the way around the pool, staring into the murky green water as he went. Even though Richmond would have cleared all the leaves off the surface that day, the water was covered in a fresh layer which the bitterly chill wind was now pushing from one side of the pool to the other. He stooped to pick up the pool net.

He was halfway through clearing the surface of the water when he noticed that the pool cleaner was lying motionless at the bottom of the pool. Walking to the section where the cleaner plugged in, he bent down and took the lid off. As a child he had always hated this part of cleaning the swimming pool because it was usually where all the insects ended up but, putting old fears aside, he reached in and scooped out a clump of sodden leaves before detaching the pool cleaner. He watched as the hole that led to the main pump began to suck the water with ease. He held up the pipe to see what had caused the blockage but he couldn't see anything so he hauled the whole cleaner out of the pool and went through each ribbed tube methodically, looking for any sign of obstruction. He was on the third tube when he noticed something inside it. He shook the tube vigorously in an attempt to dislodge whatever it was. Water and leaves flew out, splashing his shirt, and then something flew past him, landing with a dull thud on the grass. Chris turned around. When he realised what he was looking at he almost lost his balance.

It was the head of Maia's Barbie doll.

He remembered the little girl showing it to him proudly and telling him what a mermaid was. The cursed thing had even haunted him in his dreams. Bile filled his mouth and tears started to his eyes.

The rest of the doll was still inside the tube and he groped it out with his fingers. He walked over and picked the head up by its sodden hair and twisted it back onto the body. The doll was almost completely colourless, the green and gold spangles of the mermaid's tail long gone. He knelt by the side of the pool and tried to get his breathing under control. Then he got to his feet and walked to the bottom of the garden. The sun had just dipped below the horizon, bathing the garden in the soft hues of twilight. When he reached the herb garden he looked over his shoulder to see if Michelle or Rachel were there.

He was alone.

Dropping once more to his knees, he used his hands to dig a hole in the ground. He placed the doll inside and covered it with the loose dirt. When he was finished he found that he was crying.

We're all broken, Chris thought to himself as tears rolled down his face, *every single one of us. We're these broken vessels trying to find a way to undo the damage caused by the things we've done while trying to avoid doing them again. And the sad thing is that we keep doing it. We keep breaking things.*

Rachel stepped up to the Money Market counter, her envelope in her hands. She had R1 000 to send to her parents, enough to keep them for the month if combined with the profit from the bread her mother sold at the market. Her father's income these days was erratic. Many of the fishermen in Inharasso chose to repair their own nets in order to save money. Her parents could no longer rely on him bringing any money in.

Rachel greeted the plump woman handling her transaction and picked up the form that she knew by heart. She could fill in the information that was needed to transfer money with her eyes closed.

'Inhassoro again?' the woman asked.

Rachel nodded, surprised that she remembered, and continued to fill in the form.

'Where's the little one today?'

Rachel looked up, unsure how to answer the question. If she told the woman the truth, then she would have to deal with the awkward condolences and conversation that was bound to follow. On the other hand, every lie she told about Maia was like a gradual erosion of the memory of her daughter. She toyed briefly with her options.

'She's at school today,' she said, handing the form to the assistant, who began to count out the money.

'On a Saturday?'

'It's a sport thing that the children do,' Rachel lied. 'She's running a race.'

The woman continued to process the transfer. When she was finished counting the money she placed it in the cash drawer. Rachel looked around while she waited. Her heart gave a lurch when she saw Maia's friend Abigail from the nursery school walking into the store with her mother. Monique was pushing a trolley and they were coming straight towards her. Rachel turned away, keeping her head down.

'There you go,' the assistant said, looking at her curiously. She handed Rachel her receipt.

'Thank you.' Rachel grasped the piece of paper, hiked her handbag up on her shoulder and made for the exit, her head still bowed.

Michelle's head was pounding as she opened the medicine kit and took out a bottle of Panado. She popped two tablets into her mouth and chased them down with a glass of water, cringing as the medicine travelled down her throat. She had never been good at swallowing tablets as a child and found that as an adult she still needed a full glass of water to get a single vitamin or tablet into her system.

Time had passed slowly and even though she was now past the halfway mark in her pregnancy the hours spent at home were dragging. A person could only read so many books, she'd discovered, and she often found herself just walking around the house looking for things to keep her occupied.

She put the glass in the sink and leaned against the marble counter as she waited for the painkillers to take effect. She closed her eyes and breathed in deeply, her tight belly pushing against the counter. She had started to show recently and when she looked at the unattractive clothes she now had to wear it made her sigh. She wasn't as bad as some of the other mothers she saw on her visits to Dr Pieterse or the antenatal classes, but that didn't make her feel any better about her change in dress size.

The changing hormones in her body were also making it difficult to approach the matter rationally. As far as she was concerned, she had become fat, ugly and boring, qualities that she had spent a lifetime striving not to be.

'I'm sorry about earlier,' Chris said. He had come up behind her without her hearing him. He put his hands on her hips. 'We don't need to find out.'

'No, I reacted badly,' Michelle said. She rested her back against her husband's chest.

Chris started to kiss her neck, pulling her body closer to his. She could feel him against her back. When she realised what he was trying to do she pulled forward, away from him. Chris stopped.

'I'm just … tired,' Michelle said, looking down at her hands.

'And you have a headache,' Chris said sardonically. 'I know.'

He let go of her and they stood in an uncomfortable silence. Michelle tried to decide whether she was being unreasonable. It had been a few weeks since they'd had sex and she knew it was probably frustrating for Chris. Since he was giving in about finding out the baby's sex, she supposed she did kind of owe him. She turned around to face him and began unbuttoning her shirt.

'Not now,' Chris said, stopping her hands.

'What's wrong?' Michelle said. 'It's okay.'

'I've heard people get more excited for root canals.'

'Come on, Chris.'

'Don't worry,' Chris said, taking her face in his hands. 'We're both tired.'

He leaned forward and kissed Michelle on the forehead. Then he turned and walked out of the kitchen.

The touch of his kiss lingered on her skin and Michelle closed her eyes, allowing the weight of the day to wash over her. She knew that Chris was trying to bring some form of normalcy to their lives but she was just too tired to help him. All she wanted to do was to go to sleep and wake up to how things were before – before things fell apart.

Chris lay lengthwise on the couch and turned on his iPad. There was a photograph of Anja in front of a new car at the top of his Facebook feed. She was sitting on the bonnet of a Volvo with a huge smile on her face and a glass of champagne in her hand. She appeared to be toasting the salesman who was standing next to her.

My new Volvo! #sexonwheels #grrrr

Chris grinned.

We're clearly paying you too much #no13thcheque

He waited for Anja to answer and, sure enough, the iPad pinged a few seconds later.

Nooooo!!! :) LOL

Chris liked her comment and returned to his timeline to see what the rest of his network had been up to that day. The tablet pinged again and he saw that Anja had sent him a private message.

Make sure you don't leave the Durban plans at home again, Boss! :)

Ja, ja, Missy, Chris typed back. *Just make sure my coffee is ready when I get into the office tomorrow morning.*

Anja responded with an emoticon of a cup of coffee and a smiley face and Chris, chuckling, sent back one of a thumbs up. He was about to type something else when he looked up and saw Michelle in the doorway.

'I'm going to bed,' she said. She was already in the old tracksuit she had taken to sleeping in this winter.

'I'll be there in a few,' Chris replied. 'Just answering a couple of emails.'

chapter 10

MICHELLE RAISED HER eyes to the projection on the screen in front of her to follow the words to the hymn the congregation was singing. Even though she had sung Amazing Grace for most of her life, she only knew the first chorus by heart and always needed help with the rest.

She and Chris had been attending this church for about four years and they had integrated into the (mostly white, professional) community fairly easily, something she credited to Chris's ability to make friends with anyone. She, on the other hand, always struggled to form relationships with new people, especially with women, but she had pushed through and now she was part of a group of women that met weekly to talk about life, faith and family.

The venue was a relatively new building and it had comfortable chairs, classy finishings and a stage at the front of the church hall which was the platform where preachers ministered and musicians played their instruments. The stage was lit by coloured lights and a spotlight over the large screen which displayed the words to the hymns and, occasionally, videos. In Michelle's opinion it was a little too 'rock concert' for a Sunday morning but she had come to terms with the fact that the morning rituals would start with loud music and bright lights. The band was made up of drums, keyboards, a few electric guitars, a violin and a 20-voice choir. The band performed passionately as they led the congregation in song.

Michelle looked over at Chris and saw that he had his eyes closed, enjoying his time singing to God. This ability to get lost in God's presence was yet another difference between the two of them. Chris was able effortlessly to enter this state of being and he could sing for hours on end without getting bored, while Michelle could last for about ten minutes before her mind started to wander.

When a visiting preacher once said he thought heaven would be a place where they'd spend eternity engaging with Christ this way, Michelle couldn't help but hope he was wrong. She could imagine nothing worse than this kind of eternity.

She, on the other hand, preferred hearing the Bible expounded by an articulate preacher and could easily follow a two-hour sermon, where Chris would glaze over during the introduction to the message. She had woken her husband up a few times after he had fallen asleep during a sermon and often found that he was completely unable to recall what the preacher had spoken about after a meeting. But, she figured, between the two of them they probably got the best of both worlds.

As the hymn reached the third verse, predictably Michelle's mind began to wander, moving from the to-do list for the week ahead, the meetings she had lined up with clients, to the thing that had occupied her thoughts constantly for the last few months.

A baby.

Most of their friends were on their second or third children by now and, while Michelle knew perfectly well that you didn't have children because your friends were having them, there was a part of her that had started to long for a child. She and Chris were missing out on a part of life they only had a brief window of time in which to access and, with each month that passed, she knew that the window was getting smaller and smaller.

As Pastor Anton took to the stage, Michelle's eyes scanned the congregation until they came to rest on a woman two rows in front of her. She was holding a baby girl in her arms. The child must have been about six months old and she was looking over her mother's shoulder, studying the faces of the worshippers behind her with open curiosity. Every now and then her eyes would blink and close sleepily and she would jerk her small head back up. Michelle couldn't help smiling.

'*Do you see this woman?*' Pastor Anton said into the microphone, reading from a Bible app on his tablet. '*You did not give me any water for my feet, but she wet my feet with her tears and wiped them with her hair.*'

Tired from the effort of keeping her head up, the baby rested on her mother's shoulder. Suddenly her eyes locked on Michelle's. When Michelle smiled directly at her the little girl's eyes lit up and she lifted her head back up again. She gave Michelle a big smile before burping and hiccuping and bringing forth a mouthful of milk onto her mother's shoulder.

'*You did not give me a kiss,*' continued Pastor Anton, '*but this woman, from the time I entered, has not stopped kissing my feet. You did not put oil on my head, but she has poured perfume on my feet.'*

Michelle suppressed a laugh as she watched the exasperated mother shaking her head and wiping ineffectually at her shirt with a tissue. The woman handed the baby to her husband so that she could go and clean herself properly. The man took his baby daughter in his big hands and held her up to his face. He spoke silently to her and made funny faces. Michelle could see Chris doing that if they had a baby.

'Therefore, I tell you, her many sins have been forgiven, as her great love has shown. But whoever has been forgiven little, loves little.'

Michelle was aware of Pastor Anton's voice but realised she hadn't listened to a single word of the reading. It was too late now so she closed her eyes and whispered a private prayer to God, asking him to give them a child.

'We are all called to forgive our enemies, just as Christ forgave us! A-men!'

Rachel pulled Maia by the hand as the two of them entered the Christ Embassy Sunday meeting, late but barely noticed by the worshippers who were already singing and dancing with great enthusiasm. Pastor Enoch was standing on the stage shouting into the microphone and the congregation responded with great gusto.

'AMEN!'

The church met in an old shopping centre that had been stripped of its shelves and converted into a hall large enough to accommodate 2 000 people. Plastic chairs were set out in uneven rows and a makeshift stage had been erected at the front. A blaring speaker system brought music and the word to the congregation and the walls were decked with banners proclaiming 'Jesus is Lord' and 'King of Kings'.

The congregation was comprised mostly of black people, everyone dressed in the best clothes they owned. Maia always wore her white dress to church, which Rachel had found at a second-hand shop in town, while Rachel would come to the meetings in a black, ankle-length skirt and a bleach-white blouse. She had seen some churches where the worshippers came in casual clothes but she believed that if you would wear a suit when you visited with the President, you should do the same when you met with Jehovah.

'We don't forgive our enemies when we feel like forgiving them!' Pastor Enoch declared passionately. 'We forgive them because it is the only way to be set free! A-men!'

'AMEN!' the congregation shouted back as the keyboard player thumped his keys in the background.

She scanned the busy hall. She saw Tapiwa in the section where they usually sat, waving at her to come through. Rachel and Maia made their way through the crowd towards her, and Tapiwa shifted up so that they could take the two chairs she had saved for them.

'The taxi was running late,' Rachel explained as she greeted her friend. The two women wasted no time in joining in the singing. When Rachel glanced down, she saw Maia whispering to the Barbie doll Abigail had given her. She had told the child to leave it at home but somehow she had snuck it past her. She considered taking it away but didn't want to deal with a crying child in the meeting and so she let Maia be.

Even though Rachel did not understand the words of the song, she knew them by heart and understood what they meant, thanks to a translation by Tapiwa. They sang songs in a mix of languages at this church, catering to the many African nationalities that made up the congregation.

Her first visit to Christ Embassy had happened three years ago and had come about from an invitation from Tapiwa. They had met a few weeks earlier when Tapiwa had started working on the same street as Rachel, and when she suggested Rachel and Maia join her one Sunday, they'd gone along. The church was in the suburb of Randburg and it required a taxi and 30 minutes of walking to get there but, as Rachel soon discovered, it was worth the effort.

With no support or family in Johannesburg, Rachel's first year in the city had been incredibly lonely, something that had been relieved by the weekly church meetings. She had found a sense of belonging when she sang with the group of believers and her heart filled with purpose when she heard the scriptures preached from the front of the huge hall. She had even met the occasional Mozambican in a meeting and she could barely describe the joy that came from being able to speak her mother tongue to another adult.

'Pass the doll to me,' Rachel whispered in Maia's ear. 'You can get it at the end of the meeting.'

Disappointed but obedient, Maia handed the Barbie with the mermaid tail over to Rachel, sighing exaggeratedly as she looked ahead at the stage. A smile on her face, Rachel shook her head and pushed the doll into her handbag before greeting the woman seated on the other side of her daughter.

Pastor Enoch was in full cry this morning.

'Not forgiving someone is like swallowing poison and believing that the person who hurt you will die! A-men!'

'AMEN!'

'God is good!'

'All the time!'

'All the time!'

'God is good!'

'A-men.'

Pastor Enoch paused as he caught his breath. 'Sister Mary is going to lead us in a song,' he announced, 'while we take up the tithe and offering. Remember, brothers and sisters, the word of God says that if you want to be blessed, you must be a blessing.'

Then he proceeded to tell them for ten minutes about how giving to the church would welcome blessing into their own lives before he finally made way for Sister Mary to pick up the microphone and start singing. Ushers got up from their seats and started passing collection baskets down the rows, watching vigilantly to make sure no one stole from them.

Between Maia starting nursery school and her father not being able to earn very much from repairing fishing nets, it had been a tough month for Rachel and she contemplated allowing the offering basket to pass her by, torn between her obligation to her faith and the reality of her financial situation. She listened to the words of the pastor as he reinforced the scriptures, promising her that if she was generous to God then God would be generous to her. She closed her eyes and decided to stretch her faith, telling God that she would step up but that she needed him to help her with the mountain she was facing.

She opened her purse and took some money out, placing a R2 coin in Maia's eager hand and folding a R20 note in her own. When the collection basket reached them she placed her tithe inside and held the basket out for Maia to add her contribution. The little girl took her time and, when she did add her tithe, it was as though she were throwing a coin into a wishing-well. The basket moved on down the row and Maia, a big smile on her face, looked up at Rachel and blew a kiss at her. Then she stretched up to whisper in her mother's ear.

'I asked for princess hair, Mama,' she said.

The words of Pastor Anton's sermon went straight over Chris's head, a mix of scripture that he struggled to process at ten in the morning. He had his iPad in his hands, the Bible app open to the scripture that was being referenced, but the words were just a blur to him.

In a time before tablets and smartphones people used to sit with Bibles on their knees and the air would be filled with the sound of pages fluttering as the congregation searched for the relevant verse. When he and Michelle were dating they used to silently race to see who could find the verse first, the loser receiving a pinch on the leg which the rules said they had to take without drawing attention to themselves.

Michelle preferred paper to a tablet in church and she usually had her notebook out, scribbling down points that resonated with her from the message, but this morning she seemed lost in thought. Swallowing a yawn, Chris leaned forward and exited the Bible app and went through to Facebook, giving a quick look around to see if anyone had noticed. Michelle hadn't, but he could see she wasn't paying attention to Pastor Anton either. Her gaze was fixed somewhere just ahead of where they were sitting, a small smile playing about her lips. Chris scrolled through the Facebook timeline, looking at the activities of his friends who weren't in church meetings that morning.

Today had been booked off in the calendar for him and Michelle to make a baby. It was the height of Michelle's fertility window and she had set aside the afternoon for them to have sex. Devoid of spontaneity, the whole set-up felt about as passionate as two dogs at the breeders whose owners stood to the side waiting for them to do what needed to be done. It was the seventh time they had gone through this and it wouldn't have felt as cheap were it not for the fact that these days Michelle didn't show much interest in sex outside of the sacred fertility window. Chris was becoming more like a tool than a person and, as he sat back and tried to stay awake, he hoped to God that this would be the last time they would have to go through this.

chapter 11

RACHEL STARED AT the tiny brass urn, its polished surface reflecting the light that streamed in from the large windows of the Jordaans' church. It was the first time she had been in a church that looked like this but she was not in a frame of mind where she was able to appreciate the beauty of the structure. She looked up from the urn, still unable to comprehend that Maia was inside of it. In normal circumstances cremation would not have been her first choice but, given that she wanted eventually to bury Maia in Mozambique, she knew that she had had no other option. Chris had recommended it to her and, after signing the necessary papers at the crematorium, she had watched as Maia's body was wheeled through one door in a casket and the little brass urn was brought from another. Rachel switched her gaze from the urn to a large canvas a few metres away that was propped up on a wooden art easel.

The canvas was a print of one of Maia's class photographs, taken last year when she had just been enrolled at Jollyjammers. A warm smile was spread across her face and her hair was done up in two small pigtails, a style that she had asked for after seeing all the other girls at school with pigtails. Below her smiling face were two lines Rachel had never in her life expected to read:

Maia Nyaga

2009 – 2014

A tear ran down Rachel's cheek and she slowly wiped it away, turning to Tapiwa for another tissue. She was sitting in the front row, flanked by Tapiwa and Maria, who had managed to get the day off so that they could be with her. They were the only 'friends and family' she had in Johannesburg, a realisation that made her suddenly miss her mother with a searing ache.

Chris and Michelle were seated a few rows behind them, their presence an awkward necessity since it was Chris who had managed to get permission for them to use one of the side halls of the church the Jordaans attended. One of the pastors had agreed to perform the ceremony and Michelle had printed out the canvas with Maia's photo on it that morning.

Rachel didn't process a single thing that came from the pastor's mouth, his words floating over her head and passing through the echoing hall like a breath of empty wind. He had asked her if she had wanted to say anything but she had declined, knowing that she had said all she needed to say to her child at the crematorium. To Rachel this was just a ritual that needed to be completed for completion's sake.

The pastor finished the ceremony and stepped down to extend his condolences to Rachel. Tapiwa took her arm and Maria gathered up their things, neither of the women speaking. Rachel picked up the urn. It was heavier than it looked. Maria handed Rachel's bag to Tapiwa to carry, and walked back and lifted the canvas from its easel. Then she led the way out of the building.

As the women walked past Chris and Michelle, who hadn't yet moved from their seats, Rachel stopped to thank them for the hall. They were empty words, they all knew that, but it made the interaction between them a little bit manageable. Michelle had avoided all eye contact from the moment she had arrived, while Chris had tried to shield his wife with his body and draw attention away from her.

The Jordaans had arranged for a driver to transport Rachel and her two friends. He was standing at the door, waiting for their instructions, and Rachel was vaguely aware of Maria saying something to him.

In the back seat of the Toyota Corolla that would take them home, Rachel sat sandwiched between Maria and Tapiwa, Maia's ashes positioned securely on her lap. The driver started the car and the melancholic sounds of a gospel choir strained through the crackling speakers, covering the silence in melody. As they drove out the church parking lot Rachel looked back and saw Chris and Michelle standing beside their car. Tears were running down Michelle's face and Chris appeared to be comforting her. She turned back around. Tapiwa felt for her fingers and held Rachel's hand loosely in hers.

They drove through the streets of Johannesburg until they reached the Jordaan house. Rachel did not have a remote to open the electronic gates so the driver pulled up at the kerb, where he put the car into neutral, giving the three women time to get their things together. He gave Rachel a solemn nod, then put on the Toyota's indicator and pulled off into the street.

The late afternoon sun bathed the women in gold as they turned to face each other to say their farewells.

'What are you going to do with her?' Maria asked, handing Rachel the canvas before hugging her.

'I'll take her to Inhassoro when I go back.'

'I still think you should tell your parents,' Tapiwa said.

'There's nothing they can do from there and if they know they will only try to come and help, which will cost money that we don't have. I will tell them when I go back.'

The women stood in silence, accepting Rachel's decision.

'What happens now?' Tapiwa asked.

'We haven't spoken about it yet.'

'What do you want to do?' Maria asked.

'I don't know.' Rachel held the urn against her chest. 'If I leave, I lose my home, my income, my visa, and I won't be able to take care of my parents.'

Tapiwa stepped forward and hugged her. Maria followed suit again, rubbing Rachel's back this time in big comforting circles. Then Rachel opened the side gate and walked down the driveway to her room, not looking back. Once inside, she laid the canvas on the table and stood the brass urn in front of it. She pulled out a chair and sat down. She stared at the urn, the small receptacle that now contained the ashes of her child.

The choice she had to make was not a complicated one; in fact it was quite simple. It was just difficult.

Looking over to the kitchen area, she saw the dishes from the previous week, piled up and dirty. She stood up and walked over. She put the plug into the hole in the sink, turned on the tap, and poured a little dishwashing liquid into the stream of hot water. She stood and watched as bubbles started to form. Then she put the dishes in one by one and started to wash them, her empty eyes gazing out the window into the driveway as night began to fall.

The pile of dirty dishes seemed to have grown by itself. All of the surface area beside and on the kitchen sink was occupied and – Michelle couldn't deny it any longer – there was a distinctly unpleasant smell coming from that corner too. Resigning herself to the fact that she would have to do some cleaning if she and Chris were going to have plates to eat off, she cast around helplessly. Bending, she opened the cupboards below the sink and poked her head inside, then straightened up again, sighing despondently.

'What's wrong?' Chris was at the window looking out into the garden. The surface of the infinity pool was looking scummy.

'We don't have any tablets for the dishwasher.'

'Don't worry about it. I'll pick some up tomorrow.'

Michelle accepted that they could probably last another day and she switched the kettle on, opting instead to have something hot to drink. She didn't much feel like dinner anyway.

'Tea?' she offered.

Chris was sitting at the table in the breakfast nook now, scrolling through messages on his iPhone.

'Yes, please,' he replied without looking up.

Michelle opened the cupboard where they stored their crockery but found empty shelves staring back at her. How had that happened? Irritably, she closed the cupboard door, hard enough to cause Chris to look up.

'What's wrong now?'

'What are we going to do, Chris?' Michelle turned to face him, trying to hold back tears of frustration.

'Let's just have some tea and talk things through,' Chris said. He put his iPhone down and stood up to help her.

'We can't have tea,' Michelle said, pointing accusingly at the cupboard door. 'Don't you get it? There are no more clean mugs.'

Chris wasn't sure whether to laugh or not, but he knew better than to point out the obvious. This was definitely not the time to talk logistics.

'Um ...'

'I'm going to bed.'

'No, no, no,' Chris said, stepping forward and blocking Michelle's exit. 'Just sit down and let me handle things.'

Too tired to resist, Michelle slumped onto the chair Chris pulled out for her and watched as he went through the row of cupboards above the counter tops. He glanced back at her, his eyes twinkling, but Michelle wasn't in the mood. Even when he pulled out a wine glass and a gravy boat and put them on the counter with a flourish she didn't raise a smile.

'You can't drink tea fr…' Michelle protested when she realised what he was doing.

Chris ignored her. He placed a teabag into each of the containers, poured in hot water from the kettle, and then carried them across to the table, where he added milk and sugar.

'Glass or gravy boat, madame?' he asked solemnly.

Michelle smiled weakly and reached for the gravy boat, lifting it to her lips and blowing on the hot tea. Chris went back to the cupboard and extracted a packet of ginger biscuits which he brought back to the table. Then he pulled his chair close to Michelle's and leaned in to whisper into her ear.

'It was an accident.'

'I know,' Michelle said automatically.

'It was an accident,' Chris repeated, not moving away from her.

'I know, Chris.' Tears threatening, Michelle set her chin defiantly and tried, but failed, to look at him.

'It was an accident.'

Tears started to roll down Michelle's cheeks. She hated crying. Chris knew how much she hated crying.

'It was an accident,' Chris said again, tenderly kissing her hand and holding onto it before she could pull it back. He waited for Michelle's breathing to steady.

'I just wish I could go back to that moment and change it,' Michelle said, wiping roughly at her face. 'Just change one thing so that it wouldn't have happened.'

'I know.'

They sat in silence while Michelle's tears ran their short course. She blew her nose loudly into a tissue. Then she picked the gravy boat up by its handle and took a sip of her tea. Her composure returning, she turned her face to her husband.

'You know we need to talk to her,' she said.

Chris nodded.

'I'll call Riaan tomorrow and find out what the legalities are.'

Rachel lay on her bed in her nightgown and two pairs of socks on her feet, listening to the night sounds of the suburbs. Where once, long ago it seemed, she had fallen asleep to waves and tavern music, she had never got used to how little noise there was here at night. Aside from the occasional car driving past or police siren, the suburbs were void of noise, the thick trees swallowing whatever sound there was. In summer there was the buzz and clicking of insects in the garden but in winter everything was hard and still.

She didn't even have Maia's heavy breathing to mask the loneliness anymore.

It had been six days. For the first time since Maia's passing, Rachel was truly alone. The last week had been filled with funeral arrangements and the presence of Maria and Tapiwa who had managed to come by every day. Chris had also been a constant companion, helping her with all the police and hospital administration as well as the setting up of the cremation and the service at his church.

Michelle had spent most of her time inside the house, receiving visits from her friends, who brought with them flowers and food for Rachel, which she in turn had shared with Maria and Tapiwa. Rachel had only met Michelle's friends, these women in her employer's life, in passing and she was touched by their kindness.

Maia's nursery school had sent Rachel a book that the children had made for her, a collection of crayon drawings each of them had done of Maia. The teacher had had the drawings bound together and had written a letter to Rachel, expressing her condolences as well as sharing her memories of Maia from her short time at Jollyjammers.

Rachel picked up the book now and read the letter from Maia's teacher once more. It said that Maia was a joyful girl, one who was quick to share her things with others and make friends with new children. She added that Maia loved to play with the dolls in the toy box and that she had a beautiful singing voice. The theme song from *Frozen* had been her favourite.

The book had been accompanied by a gift basket with chocolates, soaps and candles, as well as all of the art Maia had done. Rachel flipped through the simple drawings, the bright colours jumping from the pages. The teacher would title each of the drawings with a marker pen, showing the parents what the theme for that day's project had been. The drawings told stories of princesses in castles and trips to holiday destinations that Maia must have heard about from the other children. One of the drawings under the title 'My Family' showed Maia standing between a mother and a father as they walked along the beach. The three of them were holding hands and had big smiles on their faces. The sun in the corner of the page was also smiling as it shone down on a picture-perfect family that existed only in Maia's imagination.

A tear rolled down Rachel's cheek and landed on the drawing, the moisture causing the watercolour pencil to dissolve and run. Rachel put the book down, wiped her face and reached over to turn off the lamp.

chapter 12

RACHEL ADJUSTED HER weight on the cheap plastic chair she had been sitting on in the Home Affairs office for the past two hours. Her back hurt. It was just after lunch and those of the fluorescent lights that were working flickered noisily in the dingy room. She had arrived at the unkempt building at sunrise and had stood in line outside for three hours with about 50 other foreigners who were applying for or renewing the visas that allowed them to live and work in South Africa.

Once inside the building she had filled out her forms before making her way to the floor where the processing of work permits was handled. She took a seat with the rest of the crowd and waited as the queue inched closer and closer to the three uninterested-looking officers who had been tasked with the processing of permits for the day.

Rachel clutched her papers and purse tightly, looking to see who was seated on either side of her. Some of these people, having travelled from neighbouring towns, had arrived the previous night and had ended up sleeping in the streets outside the property so that they could be the first in line to get their status extended. It was a dangerous choice, given the crime in the area, but it was one many people were forced to make. Rachel had done it once herself and ever since then had done everything in her power to make sure she wouldn't have to take that risk again.

This was also an environment she didn't want Maia to experience, a place that would show her where they really fit in the hierarchy of this world that her daughter knew as home.

'Next.'

Rachel looked up and saw that one of the officers, a pudgy black man with a plastic badge that read 'Thomas Mabuza' pinned to his shirt, was looking at her through the glass window that separated him from the foreigners. Quickly scooping up her things, she approached the counter and slid her papers, passport and money through the gap in the glass. Officer Mabuza picked up the papers and began to flip through them slowly, squinting up at Rachel when he got to her passport photograph. He proceeded to pick up her employment letter and read through it.

Then he asked her a question in Zulu, a tactic Rachel had often observed the officers employ to try and intimidate applicants who, like her, could not understand the language.

'I'm sorry, sir,' she responded in English, trying her best to appear submissive. 'I don't speak Zulu.'

It was all a power play. She knew that the worst thing she could do was challenge the officer's authority or appear rude. She watched as Officer Mabuza sucked his teeth and stared down at the employment letter for much longer than was surely necessary.

'How long have you been working for the Jordaan family?' he asked again, switching to English this time.

'Four years.'

Rachel could see he was about to ask another question when all of a sudden the air was filled with shouting and commotion. Behind her three officers were busy dragging a crying woman through the waiting room to where Rachel knew there was a holding cell. The woman was resisting, crying out in Portuguese, begging them not to take her, but the three men ignored her pleas, pulled the woman into the room and closed the door behind them. Her cries could still be heard in the waiting room. Rachel turned back to face Officer Mabuza, trying to remain calm and put what she had just witnessed out of her mind.

The officer smiled as he said something in Zulu to his co-worker in the next cubicle and the two men laughed at what Rachel could only assume was a derogatory joke about the woman. He picked up a rusty office stamp and marked her paperwork with ink, the sound of the impact on the page loud and authoritative. Without saying another word, he slid the papers and Rachel's passport back through the glass, motioning for her to move on.

She had six more months.

chapter 13

RACHEL WALKED DOWN the tree-lined street towards the Jordaans' house, the winter sun shining through the bare branches that were usually so lush and heavy with leaves during the summer. She was laden with groceries and the handles from the plastic supermarket bags cut painfully into her palms. She ignored the pain and continued to walk steadily, at the same time running through the list of chores that still awaited her.

Winter had journeyed past its coldest point and Rachel was looking forward to the change in season that would come in the next month. Already the sun was rising later in the day but this had done little to take the bitter cold of the season with it.

It had been five months since Maia's funeral.

Michelle and Rachel had slipped into an awkward routine, which ranged from simple greetings at the beginning and end of the day to communication around the chores that were required of Rachel. The rest of their time in the same space was spent on separate sides of the house, with Michelle spending most of hers in the study and Rachel cleaning the study and the rest of that side of the house when Michelle went out to the shops, to meet up with one of her friends or to antenatal classes.

Rachel was about five minutes from the house when the weight of the bags became too much and she was obliged to stop. She rested the bags on the ground while she massaged her palms. Looking up, she realised that she had stopped at the park she and Maia used to go to on the weekends and sometimes in the late afternoon after she was finished for the day and Maia needed to work off some energy. She hadn't been to the park in months. As she waited for the numbness in her hands to subside, she watched the handful of people who were in the park on this cold day.

A young couple were tossing a ball to their dogs, two animals that looked as though they had been rescued from a squatter camp and given a new life that none of their counterparts had been afforded. Some teenagers were throwing a frisbee to each other on the far side of the park, while a group of adults sat on the benches and watched as their children played on the swings, slides and jungle gyms. They all looked so content, enjoying the weak sun and each other's company.

Rachel bent down to pick up the plastic bags when something else caught her attention, causing her to stop dead in her tracks. Climbing up the ladder to the slide with her back to Rachel was a little girl in a blue corduroy jacket and scarf. She had tiny black pigtails sticking out from the sides of her head.

Rachel's heart beat wildly. She tried to take a few deep breaths but it hurt her chest.

The child climbed to the top of the ladder and got onto the slide, her face hidden from Rachel's view as she sat down and pushed herself forward. The air filled with a joyous scream and glimpses of small legs and flashes of blue. Rachel couldn't help it. She took a step forward, her mind telling her that it wasn't possible but her heart convincing her that it could be. The little girl climbed off the slide, still laughing, and turned to go up once more. She came running towards Rachel as though she was coming to greet her.

It wasn't Maia. Of course it wasn't Maia.

Picking up the shopping bags, Rachel walked quickly away from the park, glancing once over her shoulder to see the child and her mother, an elegant woman in skinny jeans, close together near a bench. The mother was handing her a juice box, bending to tighten her scarf ...

Rachel walked as fast as she could, the heels of her shoes striking the sidewalk and filling the air with a sharp, urgent sound. By the time she reached the side gate at the Jordaans' house she was shaking and she struggled to get the key into the lock to let herself in. She ran down the path to her room, the heavy bags almost making her stumble, with a wave of sadness moving through her unlike anything she'd felt before. She recognised it as a longing for her child that was deeper than her soul.

Safe inside her room, Rachel leaned against the door. The bags dropped from her hands.

She was alone. So completely alone. There was no one to love or love her back. She was stuck in this fortified city, living amongst people who knew only how to be served. Until this moment she had been able to look beyond this cold reality because she was here for a greater purpose – to give her child a chance to be anyone she wanted to be, and her parents the chance to survive. But now she felt well and truly trapped, with no means of escape, the noose around her neck growing tighter with every day that passed.

Mixed in with the grief and desolation, she found another emotion. It was disgust. She was disgusted with herself, with her lack of pride and her ability to accept where she was. She wished she had the courage to take her life. Love for her parents and her fear for their well-being were the only things that kept her from doing so.

This was her lot then: an educated woman who cleaned for the woman who had let her daughter die.

Michelle closed the front door. She was sure she had heard Rachel coming in the side gate, but perhaps she'd been mistaken. She went back to the kitchen, walking a little more slowly than usual due to the size of her belly. Six months of pregnancy had taken their toll on her, from the overwhelming morning sickness that still assailed her every now and then, to extreme mood swings, to the horrible weight gain and embarrassing swollen ankles. Where some women seemed to thrive on this state of being, Michelle couldn't wait for it to be over. She wished constantly that there was a way to speed up the process.

There wasn't a chance she was ever going to do this again.

As it was the weekend Chris was around to keep her company and she sat down at the kitchen table and watched as he tore into the roast chicken he was busy carving for their lunch. After a couple of minutes spent getting her breath back, she fished out some cutlery from the drawer and a couple of plates from the cupboard, and took them across to the breakfast nook, where she laid two places. While the garlic bread was heating up in the oven, she thought she'd make a fresh garden salad.

She was happy Chris was there.

Where her life had once been a whirlwind of work and social events, it had now slowed down to a lonely pace that was lived out in a mostly empty home. Her friends all had their own jobs and commitments during the day and were it not for Rachel's footsteps through the house and the domestic sounds of house-keeping, it would have been easy to believe that she was completely alone from Mondays to Fridays. She went out for her appointments with Dr Pieterse, of course, and to antenatal classes when she could get up the energy, and occasional lunchtime salads with Karlien, but for the past couple of months, she mostly hadn't gone anywhere. She found herself counting the hours until Chris came home so that at least she would have someone to talk to. She wondered ruefully if the excitement and anticipation in her heart wasn't depressingly close to what she imagined housewives in the sixties must have felt like, waiting for hubby to come home from a hard day at the office. She grimaced at the image.

Chris placed the chicken pieces onto a serving dish and took the leftover bones to the trashcan, licking the grease from his fingers before opening the lid. The trashcan was already full. Michelle could hear Chris trying to push the bones into the bag, the trash below snapping and groaning under the pressure.

'Can't you just take it out to the outside bins?' she asked testily.

'There's still space,' Chris replied, pushing down with his fist.

'But it's food,' Michelle protested. 'The flies are going to come.'

She watched Chris thinking about whether it was worth it to argue with her and was relieved when she saw him decide against it. He grabbed the black bag out of the can and tied its ends together into a clumsy knot. Michelle held the door open for him to carry it out to the bins in the courtyard. She returned her attention to the salad, tearing up lettuce leaves and sprinkling carrots, tomatoes, croutons and seeds over them.

She placed the salad in the centre of the breakfast table, adjusted the knives and forks so that they were neatly in line, and waited for Chris to come back.

Chris walked across the driveway to the back courtyard where the refuse bins were, the heavy trashbag swinging in his hands. Michelle was becoming needier by the day and, even though she had been right about taking the trash out, her controlling nature was beginning to get to him. He lifted the lid of the nearest bin and tossed the black bag inside. The smell of food beginning to rot came up at him and made him slightly nauseous.

He stood for a minute in the courtyard, mentally preparing himself for the meal with Michelle. He was about to walk back to the house when he noticed Rachel sitting on the laundry room steps with her face buried in her arms. The sight of her pain was like a blow to his heart. For a moment he considered going across to comfort her but he stopped himself. He was probably one of the last people Rachel would want to see her grief. His eyes welled up with emotion and he waited quietly for a couple of minutes more before moving quickly across the driveway and back into the house.

Michelle had just placed the chicken on the table when she heard Chris's footsteps. He must have come in from the front door. She closed the door to the garden, shooing Hugo back outside, then busied herself with rearranging the portions on the serving dish, separating dark meat from white. She didn't turn around when she heard her husband walk into the kitchen and go across to the sink, where he opened the cupboard beneath it to retrieve the roll of bin liners.

Chris ripped a fresh trashcan liner from the roll with one fierce motion of his hand and shook it out with sharp impatient slaps, rubbing his thumb and forefinger together against the thin plastic to find the opening. Then he put it in the trashcan and closed the lid.

'Don't forget to *clean* the bin before you put in a new bag,' Michelle called out, her attention still on the table and arranging their meal.

There was silence from behind her. Then she heard the cupboard door opening again and slamming hard, followed by the distinctive hiss from the nozzle of the disinfectant spray. It was prolonged and aggressive, and she could have sworn she heard Chris kick the plastic bin.

'What's wrong?' Michelle asked, finally turning round.

'Nothing,' Chris replied.

Michelle watched him trying to find the elusive opening to the bin liner, his fingers slithering impatiently, and resisted the impulse to take it from his hands and do it herself. There was a knack to it that Chris had never mastered.

'Don't tell me you're upset because I asked you to take out the trash?' she said. She picked a piece of cucumber out of the salad and brought it halfway to her lips. 'Chris?'

'I said it was nothing.'

'It doesn't *look* like nothing,' she retorted. She popped the cucumber into her mouth, watching him.

Chris ignored the comment and continued to struggle with the black plastic bag, the elusive opening amplifying his frustration.

'Just look for the edging and you'll find the opening,' Michelle called out, her suggestion answered by a slamming door and the sound of Chris storming out of the kitchen.

'Where are you going?' Michelle called. She was genuinely confused.

'To take a *shit* if you really need to know!' Chris shouted back.

The slamming of the bathroom door echoed through the house.

Michelle stood in the silent kitchen, trying to figure out what had just happened. She jumped when the timer on the oven went off to indicate that the garlic bread was ready. Almost in slow motion, she took an oven glove from the hook beside the stove and opened the oven door. The loaf was hot and it smelled delicious. She put it on the bread board and began to cut it part-way, wincing as the crust burned her hand. She carried the board to the table in the breakfast nook, placed it next to the salad, and pulled out a seat for Chris. After a few minutes she began to dish up. She helped herself to some salad, using the silver servers they'd got as a wedding present. She pulled off a piece of garlic bread and put it on her side plate. Then she selected a couple of pieces of roast chicken, taking the white meat and avoiding the dark.

chapter 14

THE HOUSE WAS pitch dark as Michelle made her way to the kitchen. It was just before sunrise. She groped through drawers, looking for the matches.

'*Lief*?' she whispered across the room, where Chris was rubbing the sleep from his eyes. 'Where did you put the matches?'

'In the drawer by the sink,' Chris whispered back.

Michelle rummaged in the drawer and found what she was looking for. On the counter where she had put it the night before was a round pink cake with the number 5 written in white icing on top and five candles puncturing the surface. A quick look up at the LCD monitor which broadcast the feed from their security cameras told her that Rachel was walking down the path with Maia, the little girl still in her pyjamas.

'They're coming!' Michelle called out in excitement. Quickly she lit the candles, the flames filling the kitchen with a warm light. 'Do you have the present?'

'*Ja, ja,*' Chris said. He held a large box in his hands, the shiny wrapping paper reflecting in the candlelight.

Michelle picked up the cake and together they walked through to the entrance hall where they waited for Rachel to reach the front door and let herself in. They readied themselves as they heard the sound of keys jingling, taking deep breaths and trying to suppress their grins.

'SURPRISE!'

Michelle beamed as she watched Maia's eyes grow wider, her shock fast replaced by excitement as she realised what was happening. She looked up at her mother, who was also smiling broadly, and Rachel motioned for her to go inside. Maia shyly approached Michelle, who was bending down and holding the cake out to her.

Michelle started to sing the traditional birthday song and Chris and Rachel joined in. Chris ended the tune with shouts and whoops, and all three of them urged the little girl to blow out her candles. Maia took a deep breath and blew, extinguishing four of the five.

'That means you have one boyfriend,' Chris teased. 'Quickly – blow it out before it comes true.'

Maia took another deep breath and was about to blow when she realised that all of the candles were burning again. She looked up at Michelle, her face a picture of astonishment. Michelle laughed delightedly and clapped her hands. She had purchased trick candles, the ones that 'magically' re-lighted themselves once they had been blown out, and she'd been hoping they would work as they were supposed to.

'You'll have to try harder, else you'll have five boyfriends!' Michelle laughed, holding the cake closer to Maia.

Maia took one extra-deep breath and blew as hard as she could, extinguishing all five of the candles. They all watched the mischievous candles closely and, once they were sure they were out for good this time, Chris turned the house lights on and they all went through to the kitchen. Michelle put the cake on the counter and picked up Maia's gift.

Maia was still trying to take everything in. So far she hadn't been able to say a word.

'This is from your mommy and from us,' Michelle said, urging the little girl to take the box. Maia took it from her shyly. Cautiously, she pulled at the wrapping paper, clearly not at all sure how to handle the present she had been given. Michelle shook her head and knelt down beside her. She held the box steady so that Maia could open it properly.

'You've got to rip it, Maia,' Michelle instructed and she pulled on one corner of the paper so that Maia could see what she meant.

Maia looked up at her mother to see if she was really allowed to do that and, after Rachel nodded her approval, she grabbed hold of the paper and tore through it, the air filled with the sound of the wrapping paper's rapid demise. While Michelle kept hold of the box, Maia took the lid off. Inside was a sparkly blue and green dress with a satiny bodice.

'It's a *princess* dress!' Maia exclaimed. She lifted it out the box and held it against her body, enchanted. The soft cloth floated around her as she tried to get a better look at it.

Michelle smiled at Chris, who was looking almost as thrilled as Maia was. Then she glanced over at Rachel. Rachel, too, had a smile on her face but for some reason her eyes looked sad. I'm probably reading something into the situation that isn't there, Michelle thought, and she returned her attention to Maia, who was now trying to put the princess dress on over her pyjamas.

chapter 15

WHEN MICHELLE FELT the baby move for the first time she was walking to the fridge. She had felt 'bubbles' or murmuring during recent weeks leading up to this moment, but this was the first time she was certain that it wasn't gas. She stopped short and put her hands on her stomach, waiting to see if it would happen again. Rachel was behind her, rinsing dishes, and she was aware of the clang of cutlery in the sink.

By now Michelle was acutely aware that she was sharing her body with someone else, someone with his or her own desires and actions. She had often wondered whether a baby would feel as if it were part of the mother or whether it would feel like a separate entity and, based on her experience thus far, she had concluded that the answer was both. The baby and its movements were not her own, yet she suddenly felt a connection to this child as if it was as intimate a part of her as her own lungs or heart.

She felt it again, a clear movement that lasted this time for about five seconds.

A smile spread across Michelle's face as she tried to process what had just happened. Any resentment she had felt towards the baby evaporated in the instant that she became so suddenly, physically, aware of its presence as a separate being with actions of its own. She gasped in wonder. Her immediate instinct was to tell someone, but the moment passed when she heard Rachel moving in the background.

Quickly leaving the kitchen, she ran through to the study and grabbed her phone to call Chris. As she waited for the call to connect she picked up the picture from her recent ultrasound, where she had put it on the corner of her desk with the till slips from the supermarket. Chris had wanted to put it up on the fridge but Michelle had felt it would be disrespectful to Rachel.

As the call went to voicemail Michelle slipped the ultrasound in her back pocket, deciding that she would put it up on the fridge after all, once Rachel had finished in the kitchen.

'That's for me,' Anja said, making room for the waiter to set her cappuccino down on the table.

As the waiter was putting the coffee down in front of Chris his phone started ringing, caller ID telling him that it was Michelle. Switching the phone to silent, he thanked the waiter and sat back, taking in the activity at Mandela Square while Anja added sweetener to her cappuccino. A public space filled with restaurants, fountains and a large statue of Nelson Mandela, Mandela Square was a short walk from their office and had become the venue for the lunchtime outings that had become a regular occurrence over the last few weeks. Hannes and other colleagues would occasionally come along but, for the most part, it was usually just the two of them.

'Who was that?' Anja asked.

'Michelle,' Chris replied. 'I'll call her when I get back to the office.'

'I still don't know how you drink that without milk,' Anja said.

'I'm not a child that needs sugar in everything,' Chris chuckled.

'I'm sorry. We're not all on the verge of forty, old man.'

'Hey, watch it!' Chris protested. 'I'm still in my thirties.'

'Barely!'

Chris smiled and let Anja win this round of banter, a duelling of humour that had become the staple of their interaction. As he sipped his coffee, nostalgia for a time when things between him and Michelle had been like this surfaced. He couldn't remember when last –

'Otherwise? How're things?' Anja interrupted his thoughts.

'Things are okay,' Chris responded. 'It's been tough with both of them at home, but I think Michelle is handling it better now than she did in the beginning.'

'I meant with you.'

Chris paused, somewhat taken aback.

'Wow. I'm not sure how to answer that,' he said. 'You're the first person who's asked me that question in a long time.'

Having just finished cleaning Michelle's study, Rachel was on her way back to the kitchen to put the utensils away when she looked out of one of the guest room windows into the garden. Michelle was lying on a deckchair beside the pool, the book she was reading resting on her pregnant belly. Her eyes were closed and her face lifted to the late winter sun, her legs stretched out. She looked totally relaxed, lying there by the green pool that Chris hadn't yet managed to get back to its original colour.

Rachel couldn't help thinking how different Michelle's pregnancy was to how hers had been.

By this stage of her pregnancy, she had managed to secure a job with the Jordaans and was working a second job on the weekends for a family who lived two kilometres from them so that she could save up money for after the birth. The Jordaans had graciously told her they had no problem with her keeping Maia in the house while she worked on the proviso that it didn't affect her productivity and, with neither of them being in the house during the day, the arrangement had ended up working out perfectly.

She had given birth to Maia via caesarean section at the Chris Hani Baragwanath state hospital in Soweto, where she spent the night in recovery before taking a taxi back to the Jordaans' house. For a week she tried to learn how to be a mother to her first baby. Her own mother had wanted to come down from Mozambique to be with her but financially it had proven impractical and they were forced to make do with phone calls.

In the kitchen Rachel opened the fridge and took out the milk so that she could make her mid-morning tea. As she was closing it she noticed an odd black and white photograph stuck to the fridge door with a magnet. She put the milk on the counter and then walked back to the fridge and took the picture off the door. She held it up for closer inspection.

It was an ultrasound of the baby.

Rachel stared through the grey haze at the silhouette. She could make out the baby's profile. Nose, hands and feet were all clearly visible. Below the image were words and numbers detailing the progress of the child's growth and development. For some reason she couldn't put the ultrasound back on the fridge. She held it flat against her chest, her heart pounding uncomfortably. Her mouth went dry.

The ultrasound changed things.

A noise on the other side of the house startled Rachel and she shoved the photo into the pocket of her uniform. Then, walking quickly but quietly, she left the kitchen, went out the main entrance and hurried to the domestic quarters. She was practically running by the time she opened the door and bolted inside, her heart beating even harder. She sat down on her bed and took the ultrasound out of her pocket. Immediately she felt herself consumed with hot anger. She scrunched the photograph up in her hand and for a second contemplated tearing it into pieces before reason stepped in and she stopped herself.

She unfolded the damaged picture and smoothed it out as best she could. She reached under the bed and felt around for the red biscuit tin. She took out her passport and placed the ultrasound between two of its pages. Her collection of R100 notes caught her eye. The stash from Michelle's bag had continued to grow over the months and she gave a tight little smile. Then she placed the passport with the ultrasound picture inside it on top of them, pushed the lid onto the tin and slid it back under the bed. Standing up, she dusted off her uniform and returned to the house. A feeling she didn't recognise, something like a mixture of power and guilt, rampaged through her.

The kitchen was empty and she could hear no sound of Michelle. Rachel took the vacuum cleaner out of the cupboard and went through to the lounge to finish her chores for the day.

Chris's heart was pounding as he sprinted on the treadmill, the rush-hour traffic in the gym adding to his sense of urgency. He was one in a line of 20 treadmills that looked down into the Virgin Active indoor swimming pool and the majority of the runners seemed to be racing as if they were about to complete the Comrades Marathon.

He looked down at the red dial as the digits scrolled down: 35 seconds away from his goal of 10 minutes of running. Pumping his arms, he urged himself to continue as he straightened his posture and tried to focus all remaining energy into his legs, the manic speed of the music he was listening to through his headphones blaring into his ears and spurring him on.

One last burst of energy as the dial hit zero and the treadmill slowed to the 'cool down' speed. Chris inhaled painfully. His current fitness level left him out of breath for a distance and time he would have considered a mere warm-up at university. Sweat poured down his face as he picked up his towel and dabbed the moisture from his skin.

Climbing off the treadmill, he walked to the water fountain and refreshed himself, before taking out his iPhone to update the stats from his run in the Nike app he used to track his progress. He had been running for three weeks now and was slowly building up his stamina. When the app congratulated him on his progress he felt absurdly pleased. His statistics safely logged, the app then asked him if he wanted to share the result of his run on Facebook and he hit 'SHARE', sending his fitness brag into cyberspace. He enjoyed posting the results of his runs online, not only because it motivated him but because it also made him feel good when he saw the ten likes from fellow runners who were approving his commitment to keeping fit.

As Hannes always joked, 'It doesn't count if it's not on Facebook.'

Walking through the busy gym, Chris was about to make his way down to the showers when his phone vibrated and he looked down to see a new notification. Anja had commented on his recent activity on Facebook.

Getting faster every day! Impressive Boss!

Chris smiled and liked her comment, then staggered down the stairs to the changing rooms.

Michelle closed the door to the garden and put her copy of Khaled Hosseini's *The Kite Runner* on the breakfast table. The warmth from the sun had left her feeling drowsy; in fact it had lulled her to sleep earlier on the wooden deckchair. A late-morning nap on the couch was ruled out when she heard Rachel vacuuming the living room and so she opted to make herself a pot of rooibos instead.

Life had slowed to a crawl for Michelle. She felt as though she was drifting, waiting for the baby to come so that she could continue living again. Her friends had stopped trying to get her to go out with them and, bar the occasional visit from Karlien, she spent most of her time alone at home. Chris had started going to gym again, so he got home later than usual from work, and sometimes he went out to drinks with his friends and came home after she'd gone to bed.

She didn't really care.

These days she would rather be alone in the house by herself than alone in the house with her husband.

Having prepared the teapot, while she waited for the kettle to boil Michelle wandered over to the fridge to get a glass of water. As she sipped, her eyes roved over the various invitations and photographs stuck to the fridge door with magnets. Chris with a paper hat on from a few Christmases ago. She and Karlien at the garden shop with a trolley load of seedlings. A blurry photo of Hugo in his basket. She was about to walk back to the kettle when she stopped, frowning. Something was missing. There was a gap where she had stuck the ultrasound of the baby. She stared at the space, confused. She looked around the kitchen and then down the side of the fridge to see if it had fallen off. Nothing. With some difficulty, she bent over to see if the image might perhaps have fallen and slipped or been scuffed underneath the fridge, but all she could see there was a lot of dust and a 50 cent coin. Using the edge of the counter to help her, Michelle pulled herself up and stood with her hands on her hips, gazing around the room. *Had* she actually put the photo on the fridge, she wondered, or was she going mad? They did say pregnant women lost their brains.

She made her tea and carried it through to the baby's room, where she stood in the doorway looking at the paint tests on the wall, the unassembled crib and the dresser that one of her friends had passed on to her. Chris had said he would paint the walls over the weekend and that together they could assemble the crib once the paint had dried.

They were going for a storybook theme for the room, with pages from some of their favourite children's books framed and hung on the walls. She had already picked out pages from *The Little Prince*, *Winnie The Pooh* and *Where The Wild Things Are* and was waiting for Chris to make his contribution from some of the books he had loved as a child. So enthusiastic at first, he had been the one to encourage her, but now it seemed to be the other way round.

Michelle proceeded to the study and turned on her computer. Out of habit, she began to check her emails. Outside of generic emails from the stores with whom she had accounts and bills that needed to be paid, there was nothing. All of her professional work had been split between her colleagues when she went on unpaid leave and in the beginning there had been lots of emails back and forth. Gradually, though, communication had slowed and then stopped. She realised that in fact she had no idea what was happening at the office and who was looking after her clients. The lack of contact left her feeling aimless, as though she had lost all her skill and value in her career. She amounted to nothing more than a baby-making machine.

Bored, she logged onto Facebook and looked around the timeline that she hadn't visited in about two months. Chris was always on the site but she found it tedious and were it not for the fact that he had set up the account for her, she probably wouldn't even have one.

The notification centre showed 67 notifications and she was about to look through them to pass some time when she noticed Chris's recent activity in her timeline. He had just finished running at the gym, apparently, but while he had registered one of his best times to date, it wasn't the speed that caught Michelle's attention.

She clicked on the post and started to read through his interaction with someone called Anja – flirty one-liners filled with smiley faces and cute hashtags.

Michelle opened Anja's profile and began to browse through her information, her eyes scanning through the dozens of photographs this woman had online for everyone to see. She learned that she was single. And anyone could see that she was extremely attractive. Who was this Anja who was shamelessly flirting with her husband? Because that was definitely what it was. But what upset Michelle more was that Chris had clearly been flirting back, and for some time.

Suddenly Michelle felt dizzy. She closed her laptop. She didn't feel like tea anymore.

Rachel was standing at the sink, rinsing the last of the dishes before she finished for the day. Her heart jumped when she heard footsteps on the kitchen tiles and she looked round to see Michelle standing behind her with an empty mug.

'Can I put this in?' Michelle asked.

Rachel, her hands deep in the hot water, nodded and waited as Michelle leaned awkwardly across her to add the mug to the rest of the dishes. Neither of the women said anything else and after a minute Michelle moved out of the way. Rachel continued rinsing the dishes and stacking them in the dishwasher. It was only when she turned the machine on that she noticed Michelle was still there, standing in the breakfast nook and staring out at the green infinity pool. Rachel dried her hands on a towel, murmured, 'I'm finished now' to her employer's back, and picked up her keys.

Michelle had been lying in the bath for about ten minutes when she heard Chris's car in the driveway. After his run he'd spent some time at the weights section at the gym with his friend Riaan and had texted ahead to tell her not to save dinner for him. She listened as he came indoors and heard him shuffling around the house, whistling a snatch of a melody she couldn't identify. She was still hurt by what she had seen earlier on Facebook but after she had read his interaction with the woman called Anja again, she couldn't tell if she was reading something into it that wasn't there.

It was difficult to read tone on that medium.

She waited a few moments until she heard Chris's footsteps coming along the passage.

'I'm in the bath,' she called out.

Chris appeared in the doorway. His face was red and his gym clothes were sweat soaked.

'Hey,' he said.

'Hey.' Michelle sat up in the bathtub. 'How was training?'

'Painful,' Chris replied as he kicked his gym shoes off. He sat down on the floor in the archway of the door.

'Guess that's how you know you're doing something right,' Michelle said, smiling tentatively.

Chris closed his eyes and exhaled, grunting agreement.

'How was work?'

'The client decided to change their minds on the final designs, which means my workload has just doubled for the week.'

Michelle processed the information and shifted her weight, the movement sending ripples across the water. Chris shuffled closer to her and put his hand on her belly. Together they watched as the baby turned, pushing off Michelle's stomach with a foot or an elbow in order to rearrange itself. Chris grinned at the action while Michelle winced.

'That was my bladder, baby,' she said, but she smiled too.

Chris gazed at her swollen belly, watching, waiting for her skin to move and Michelle smiled tiredly at him and put a hand on his damp hair. She considered asking him who Anja was. The only problem was that there was no way of doing this without sounding as if she was suspicious or, worse, had been spying on him.

'Chris,' she said suddenly, 'did you take the ultrasound photo that I stuck on the fridge?'

Chris shook his head.

'It's not there anymore.'

'Maybe it's underneath.'

Michelle was on the verge of pointing out sharply that she had already looked there, what did he think, but it had been a while since their conversations had lacked animosity and so she checked herself. She didn't want to start an argument this late in the evening.

'You're probably right,' she said. 'I'll look later.'

Rachel peered at the crumpled ultrasound image. The room was dark save for the light from her bedside lamp. She traced the outline of the baby's face and body with her finger. She hadn't been able to afford to get an ultrasound of Maia when she was pregnant and so had missed out on the wonder that came from seeing your unborn child for the first time. She had simply trusted that the doctor was telling her the truth when he told her everything was okay – not that she would have been able to tell any different with a photograph of her womb.

As she stared at the picture she started to sing a lullaby, one that her mother had sung to her as a child and that she had in turn sung to Maia. It had been the song that would always get Maia to sleep when she was a baby. It reminded Rachel of home, the village of Inhassoro and the warm, deep ocean she used to know so well. She sang it through twice and then she tucked the ultrasound under her pillow, turned off the lamp and went to sleep.

chapter 16

IT WAS FRIDAY afternoon and Rachel was doing the ironing. She pressed the wrinkles out of one of Michelle's white collared shirts, listening to the gurgle and hiss from the iron as she tilted it. Her appointment at Home Affairs to renew her visa was scheduled for Monday and she still hadn't managed to ask the Jordaans if she could leave Maia on the property while she was gone for a few hours. They were always both so busy, she scarcely ever saw them during the week.

She was just putting Michelle's shirt on a hanger when she heard footsteps in the passage. She looked up as Chris and Michelle entered the kitchen together, both of them looking down at their phones as they walked. Michelle only noticed Rachel when she was almost at the fridge.

'Rachel!' she exclaimed, smiling. 'What are you doing hiding in the corner? I would have thought you were done for the day.'

'I'm just finishing up,' Rachel said, smiling back. She took a pair of Chris's jeans out of the ironing basket.

Chris had already opened the fridge and cracked open a beer, while Michelle was setting her work things and handbag down on the counter, absentmindedly chewing on her thumbnail and reading messages on her iPhone at the same time.

'How has the day been?' Chris asked Rachel, taking a swig straight from the bottle and leaning against the counter.

'It was good. I cleaned the windows.'

'That's good. Great. Thank you,' Chris said. He already had his iPad in his free hand. He ambled over to the breakfast nook where he pulled out a chair. Michelle had her back to Rachel, her fingers typing furiously into her iPhone, and the kitchen returned to silence. Rachel had never used a smartphone. It was a source of fascination to her to see how Chris and Michelle would sit next to each other in silence for ages while they interacted with their phones and tablets.

She folded Chris's jeans and put the ironing board away. Then she went across to the breakfast nook and waited for Chris to look up. Culture and custom required that important questions were always to be asked of the male in the house.

'I was wondering if I could ask you a favour,' she began.

Michelle, who had taken a seat on one of the counter stools, looked up briefly to see what Rachel had to say, half her attention on her phone.

'What is it?' Chris asked.

'I really don't want to be an inconvenience, so please say no if you can't help me – '

'Please, Rachel,' Chris said, interrupting her, 'just tell us what it is.'

‘I need to get my visa renewed on Monday and because I don’t have anyone to look after Maia, I was wondering if I could leave her here.’

‘What about Jollyjammers?’ Michelle asked without looking up from the phone. ‘Won’t she be at school?’

‘The teachers are having a conference on Monday,’ Rachel replied. ‘She’ll stay in my room the whole time, but I just didn’t want to leave her here without you knowing about it.’

Chris turned to Michelle and started speaking to her in Afrikaans, briefly excluding Rachel from the conversation. Rachel’s eyes flickered anxiously between her two employers, trying to read their body language as they discussed the matter. Michelle didn’t look particularly overjoyed at what Chris was saying.

‘She’ll be fine in my room,’ Rachel interjected in English. ‘I just wanted to let you know so you didn’t get a surprise.’

‘No, no, Rachel,’ Michelle said, although she looked irritable. ‘You can’t leave her on her own in your room. She can stay in the house with me. I can work at home for a few hours. I just need you to be back before 1:30.’

‘Yes, of course,’ Rachel said. ‘Thank you, Michelle.’

Michelle went back to her iPhone and there was a moment of not very comfortable silence.

‘Is the employment letter that I gave you still good?’ Chris asked.

‘Yes, it is,’ Rachel replied. ‘Thank you.’

Chris nodded. With nothing left to say, Rachel picked up the pile of still-warm ironing and went off to Chris and Michelle’s bedroom to put the clothes away. She breathed a sigh of relief, grateful that she had managed to find a solution to her problem.

It was time to go and collect Maia from school. In her room

Rachel hastily pulled off her uniform and grabbed a pair of jeans hanging over the back of the chair.

'What's wrong, *lief?*' Chris asked.

'Nothing,' Michelle said, looking him briefly in the eyes before returning her attention to the message she was typing. She wasn't happy but she didn't want to get into it now, especially as they were both tired. They never argued well when they were in that state.

'I know what that means,' Chris said, laughing from across the room.

Michelle inhaled, trying, but failing, to resist the bait.

'I just don't like it when you make decisions on my behalf,' she said. 'I'm crazy about Maia, as you know, but I also have to work. If I had said no after what you said, I would have looked like a bitch.'

'Come on – I just figured you'd want to help if you could.'

'Of course I'd want to help,' Michelle said, putting the phone down and facing her husband. 'That isn't the point. I don't like it when you don't include me in the decision, that's all.'

Fully expecting Chris to fire back at her for being inflexible, Michelle set her chin defiantly.

'Okay,' Chris said, surprising her, and getting up to walk across the kitchen towards her. 'I'm sorry.'

He kissed her on the shoulder and lingered for a minute. He pulled a stray hair back behind her ear. As happy as Michelle was that he had apologised, it was patronising that he had done so without any resistance. She knew her competitive nature. She never enjoyed a victory unless it was one that was won after a good fight.

‘How are you feeling?’ Chris asked.

‘I’m fine,’ Michelle said. ‘But I wish we hadn’t gone for the test yesterday. Now we’re going to have to wait all weekend until Monday to find out.’

‘The waiting makes it worse,’ Chris agreed. ‘Remember the days when you got a new cellphone and had to wait 24 hours for it to charge before you could use it.’

Michelle smiled at both the memory and the odd comparison.

‘I don’t know what you’re talking about,’ she said, ‘because I never waited.’

Chris laughed and kicked off his shoes.

Michelle went to the fridge. She took two ready-made meals out of the freezer compartment. ‘Which one do you want for supper?’ she asked.

chapter 17

RACHEL LIFTED THE beige sofa in the TV room and moved it out of the way, pushing the vacuum cleaner beneath it so that she could reach the dirt. She vacuumed the lounge once a week but hadn't performed a 'deep clean' in months because the TV room was so rarely used by the Jordaans, in spite of Chris having bought such a big TV.

Out of sight, out of mind.

When Rachel had to have Maia in the house during school holidays, while the Jordaans were at work she would usually keep her in this room, the Disney channel distracting her enough to allow Rachel to complete her chores. Maia had loved the huge television screen and she'd asked Rachel when they were going to get one that size for their room, which had made Rachel laugh. Even if she had been able to afford one, a TV that size would have taken up their entire wall, a factor that hadn't occurred to Maia of course.

Rachel put the sofa down and dragged the machine across the room, feeding its hunger for dust and dirt with whatever lay in its path on the dirty floor. It was strange but she always found an incredible sense of satisfaction when she felt a large amount of dirt disappear into the vacuum cleaner. She liked to hear the particles scrape against the throat of the machine before they disappeared forever.

She walked to the other couch, the single-seater, and bent down to lift it, extending the mouth of the cleaner beneath it once she had its edge firmly in her hand. The dirt struggled against the suction and then something large entered the cleaner and blocked the flow. The motor strained as it tried to pull it through, making a gasping noise. She set the couch down on the floor and lifted the machine to see what was causing the obstruction.

It looked like a large piece of paper.

Rachel tugged it gently from the cleaner and turned it over, the motor quietening down to a steady hum now that the obstruction had been removed. It was an old piece of office paper, the surface covered in crudely drawn lines of crayon, giving a clear indication of who the artist had been.

It showed a mother and a daughter walking on a beach, the bright blue ocean rolling beside them while a group of stick figures stood to the side. Scattered on the beach were crudely drawn cowry shells and riding on top of the water were some boats, the distinct sails indicating that they were dhows. The mother and the daughter were holding hands, their stick bodies struggling to support their comical oversized heads.

Without planning to, Rachel sat down on the sofa. She stared at the drawing as if her eyes could burn holes in it while the vacuum cleaner buzzed aimlessly in the background.

Maia had drawn it the day she passed.

chapter 18

RACHEL WAS AT the two-plate stove stirring the porridge, while Maia sat at the table, scribbling furiously on a piece of paper with a blue crayon. The rest of her brightly coloured art kit laying scattered around her. Rachel had already warned her what would happen if she went off the page onto the table. Today Maia was wearing the sparkly green and blue princess dress Michelle and Chris had given her for her fifth birthday. She had immediately called it her mermaid costume because it was the same colour as the sea and vaguely like the tail of her Barbie doll, although Barbie's spangles were wearing off fast. At first she had tried to wear it every day but Rachel had put her foot down for the sake of cleanliness and told her that it was only allowed to be brought out on Mondays.

'That's pretty,' Rachel said, looking over her daughter's shoulder.

'It's our family,' Maia explained. 'And we're all at the sea, with

Granny and Grandpa ...'

Rachel carried the pot to the table and began to dish up their breakfast. Maia kept on drawing. She had finished the ocean and was busy drawing the beach sand now in very bright yellow, her tongue sticking out from between her lips as she concentrated on drawing a straight line.

Rachel put the empty pot back on the stove and shifted her chair beside Maia's. She pulled the sugar bowl towards her and sprinkled a tablespoon of white sugar over each of their bowls, before placing the bowl out of Maia's reach. Maia put down her crayon and they held hands and gave thanks for the meal. Then she stirred the sugar into her porridge and waited for it to cool, just as her mother had taught her.

Rachel's visa appointment at Home Affairs was at 10:30, although that didn't always mean anything. She was feeling anxious already, knowing that she had a time limit and had to be back at the Jordaans by 1.30. She had gone through all her paperwork the night before and made sure that she had the exact amount of money and that everything was in order. She had learned from experience almost every time she'd been to Home Affairs that the visa officers could be incredibly temperamental and that anything from using the wrong colour pen to not having the exact amount of change could put them in a bad mood.

'I have to go into town today, Maia,' Rachel said, blowing on a spoonful of porridge. 'Michelle said that she will look after you while she works.'

Maia nodded and copied her mother, her little cheeks puffing out as she blew on her porridge, her eyes squinting down the length of her spoon.

'You're going to have to promise me that you'll behave yourself.'

Maia nodded and opened her mouth to swallow the porridge.

'Careful, it's still hot,' Rachel said, as usual. 'Blow on it a bit more.'

Maia stopped and obediently pursed her lips.

'Can you take me to the park when you come back?' she asked.

Realising that her daughter was trying to bargain a reward for her good behaviour, Rachel had to suppress a smile.

'If the sun is still shining when I get home, then yes, I will,' she said.

Maia smiled and brought the spoon to her mouth, first looking at Rachel to see if it was time to start eating.

'That's my girl,' Rachel said and did the same.

Michelle stood in front of the espresso machine, watching the dark brown liquid trickle down into the two white mugs she had warmed up in the microwave. She drank unsweetened cappuccino in the morning, while Chris preferred his black and usually laced with sugar. He used to take it with three spoons of sugar but she'd noticed that since he'd been back at the gym, he had cut sugar out completely, something she'd never managed to get him to do. She walked over to the fridge to get some milk. The carton was there, but it was empty. She threw it in the trashcan. She carried the mugs over to the counter and sat down. At that moment Chris walked into the kitchen, laptop open, trying clumsily to proofread one of his reports. His eyes lit up when he saw the coffee and he walked over to Michelle and kissed her on the head.

'I asked you to get milk yesterday,' Michelle said.

'Are we out?'

Michelle nodded. She reached for one of the bran muffins she'd bought from the market the day before, broke off a piece and popped it in her mouth.

'I'll get some today,' Chris promised. 'Just text me to remind me.'

He closed his laptop and broke off a piece of the muffin Michelle was eating, smiling at her as he chewed.

'Anything else happening today that I need to know about?' Chris asked, his mouth full. 'Oh yes, we've got Maia this morning, haven't we?'

'*I've* got Maia,' Michelle said. '*You* are going to the office.'

'Sorry,' Chris said ruefully.

'And we've got dinner with the Elliotts at that spot in Linden ...'

'Daddy!'

Michelle turned around to see Maia running into the kitchen with a big smile on her face, her arms stretched out towards Chris. Rachel was just behind her. She looked embarrassed.

'Daddy?' Chris said, bending down to pick Maia up and give her a hug.

'I'm sorry about that,' Rachel said. 'She hears the other children at school calling their fathers "Daddy" and thinks that's what all older men are called.'

Maia beamed around the room while Chris began to tickle her, making Michelle and Rachel laugh and Maia squirm and giggle.

'Well, that's a relief,' Chris said. 'If you ever want to give a man a fright, then walk through his front door with a child he doesn't know who calls him Daddy.'

He put Maia down and slipped his laptop into its bag. He hitched the bag around his shoulder and prepared to leave. Rachel guided

Maia towards Michelle, her caretaker for the morning.

'Thank you for helping me today,' she said.

'It's not a problem,' Michelle replied.

Maia twirled for Michelle in her princess dress and Michelle smiled at her.

'Would you like to be my secretary today?' she asked.

Maia nodded enthusiastically.

'Do you know what a secretary is?' Rachel said.

With a wide smile, Maia shook her head.

'Well, that's okay,' Michelle told her. She pulled out a chair and helped the little girl up onto it. 'You just take a seat here and I'll tell you about it when your mother goes. Being a secretary is a very important job.' She smiled up at Rachel. 'I think we'll be good,' she said. 'But please just make sure you're back at 2 o'clock at the very latest.'

Rachel nodded as she gathered her things. 'Thank you again.'

'How are you getting to Home Affairs, Rachel?' Chris asked as he bent down to kiss Michelle goodbye.

'I'm going to walk to the taxi rank and then take a taxi.'

'At least let me give you a lift to the taxi rank. It's in the direction I'm heading anyway.'

'It's okay, Chris,' Rachel replied. 'I'll be fine.'

'Nonsense. You're getting a lift. Now let's go.'

Rachel hesitated. The Jordaans were already being so helpful, she didn't want to impose. Maia slid off her chair and began to push her towards Chris.

'Go, Mama, go!'

'Now that's more like it,' Chris said. 'Listen to your daughter.' He winked at Michelle and looked expectantly at Rachel.

Reluctantly, Rachel followed him to the front door, Maia tagging after them, hopping from one leg to the other.

'Remember to be home at seven, *lief*,' Michelle called out. 'We need to be there at eight …' She paused to listen if Chris had heard her, but the silence told her he probably hadn't. Maia was hovering in the doorway, chewing on the end of her sleeve.

'Why don't you jump back up here, Maia,' Michelle said, patting the chair next to her. 'You look so pretty today.'

'I'm a princess,' Maia explained, a little more solemn now that the two of them were alone.

'You certainly are,' Michelle said. 'And today you are also my secretary.'

Maia took her seat and gazed expectantly at Michelle, who reached over for the sheets of office paper she had ready. She put a pen on the table in front of her.

'A secretary helps a boss with their work,' Michelle explained, opening her laptop. 'They take notes and help them when they need things. And, when they're done with their work, they get to have a nice lunch *and* ... a fancy coffee, just like a grown up.'

Maia's eyes lit up at the mention of coffee – coffee was something her mother would never have allowed. Michelle smiled serenely back at her. She knew there wasn't a chance in hell she was really going to give Maia coffee but she had seen with her friends' children how all they really wanted to do was drink sweet milk foam from a fancy coffee cup. She was more than willing to feed that fantasy if it bought her a few hours of good behaviour.

'Let's get to work, shall we?' Michelle said with a glance at the kitchen clock.

chapter 19

MICHELLE STOOD IN the doorway to the kitchen, her back aching from her heavy belly. It was late in the afternoon and she had spent most of the day obsessing about the missing ultrasound. She had turned her office inside out and checked beneath the fridge three times. She watched Rachel wiping down the kitchen counters and her eyes narrowed slightly. There was only one other thing that could have happened to the ultrasound.

She had thought about trying just to forget about it but she couldn't. And the more she obsessed, the more frustrated she became by the fact that she was being held hostage by the guilt that existed inside her because of Rachel. In a normal situation she would have simply asked Rachel outright if she had seen the missing item but, with all that had happened in the last few months, Michelle felt guilty about everything when it came to Rachel. She couldn't even complain if Rachel hadn't emptied the dishwasher or forgotten to disinfect the outside trashcans. She couldn't question anything the maid did these days.

'Rachel, I need to ask you about something.'

Michelle watched as Rachel turned to face her, her eyes unresponsive. Michelle took a step towards her, trying to be firm without appearing confrontational.

'Have you seen the photo of the baby that was on the fridge?'

Rachel shook her head, looking back at Michelle with those tired eyes that haunted Michelle when she tried to sleep at night.

'Are you sure?' Michelle asked. 'It was stuck with a magnet on the fridge door and now it's gone. I thought that maybe it had fallen off or you had seen it when you were cleaning.'

'I haven't seen it.'

Michelle tried to read Rachel's expression or body language to see if she was being deceived. It was a stupid thing to lie about but Michelle did sense, minutely, that something was moving behind Rachel's emotionless facade.

'Okay,' she said, searching Rachel's stare one last time.

She was about to leave the kitchen when she noticed a piece of paper sticking out of the front pocket of Rachel's uniform. There was something about its texture and colour ... She stopped.

'What's that?' she asked, nodding at the pocket.

Rachel followed her gaze. She looked Michelle direct in the eyes.

'Nothing,' she said.

Michelle took a step towards her. She knew she was about to cross a line.

'What is it?' she repeated. 'In your pocket.'

Rachel stared back at her in silence, her jaw clenched, but her hand had moved to her chest and she held it against her pocket. Michelle took another step forward. Slowly, she extended her arm, her fingers outstretched. She could feel the heat of Rachel's body but Rachel did not move a muscle, except to press her hand more tightly against her chest. Michelle reached in and, the tips of her manicured nails almost brushing Rachel's cheek, she eased the piece of paper from Rachel's pocket. It slid softly past Rachel's unresisting fingers.

Rachel's whole body was quivering now but she held Michelle's gaze, hands resting by her sides, and even when her employer looked down and unfolded the paper she did not move.

Michelle knew even as she was unfolding it that she had made a huge miscalculation, but her expression remained stony. She was incapable of showing even a hint of remorse. She slowly folded Maia's cheerful ocean drawing back to its original shape and placed it on the counter next to Rachel before she turned to leave.

She heard not a sound behind her as she left the room and went to her study.

Rachel was shaking. She felt fixed to the spot as if her shoes were nailed there. Her heart pounded and her head was bursting with conflicting emotions. One of these emotions, as she was more than aware, was pure guilt. The knowledge that she had stolen the ultrasound, that moment of unexplainable impulse, had weighed heavily on her conscience at the time and it still did. Another emotion was deep, hot anger mixed with outrage. Michelle had had no right to invade her personal space and take the picture from her, no matter how justified she thought she might have been in the action (and was, although Michelle didn't know it, of course). Her mind spinning, Rachel tried to get a fix on just how far things had fallen out of control. Automatically, she picked up a dishcloth and started to wipe down the counter as she tried to process what had just happened between her and Michelle.

Was this normal? Was this how people treated each other?

She sprayed the counter with Mr Min and rubbed hard at a mark left by a piece of dried food. The stubborn stain resisted. She sprayed a jab of liquid directly on it and kept scrubbing until a wave of nausea hit her. What was wrong with her?

Michelle had just violated her privacy and her immediate response was to start cleaning the house. Where was her self-respect? When was the point when she would say enough is enough?

She wasn't some empty-headed immigrant these people could treat like a child. She was a human being, a woman entitled to respect and dignity. She and Michelle were the same age, for heaven's sake! Never in a million years had she envisioned herself in this kind of situation and, for the first time since Maia's death, she wanted to pack her bags and disappear. No one would look for her; she could just vanish. As she thought about disappearing her mind started to wander. She imagined herself leaving the gas stove on in the kitchen, striking a match and walking away as everything that Chris and Michelle held dear disintegrated – whoof! – in a single moment.

To make them feel the loss that she felt.

Chris dipped the testing kit into the green water and pulled out a sample to analyse.

'It's too acidic,' he said, turning around to look up at Richmond, who was standing behind him watching the process with feigned interest. Richmond just stared at him; the word was not contained in his lexicon of English words.

'It's ... uh ... the water is bitter,' Chris tried to explain, 'like there's poison in it.'

Richmond nodded to show that he understood but Chris was pretty sure he hadn't managed to explain it well enough. He frowned down at the pool's murkiness and tried to think of what he needed to do in order to neutralise the problem. In his mind you just added more chlorine and the problem would be solved, but they'd tried that and it didn't seem to be working.

He straightened up and shrugged. 'I'll fix it later,' he told Richmond confidently, although he wasn't confident at all. In the study he went online to search for information on how to fix an acidic pool. As he scrolled through the different options he heard the ping of a notification and opened his Facebook account. It was a comment from a random friend on a video he had posted earlier. After acknowledging the interaction with a like, he navigated his way to Anja's profile to see if there had been any new activity. There was a new photograph, one he hadn't seen before. Anja and another young woman drinking cocktails on an urban rooftop. The friend was blonde and had something about her. He clicked on the tag to open her profile.

Elize de Waal.

Blonde hair and honey skin. Like Anja's, Elize's profile had no security restrictions either, and Chris began to scroll through her photographs. She looked a little wilder than Anja, he thought. She'd be the girl who was first to order the shooters, and the girl who closed down the club. He arrived at some photographs of her on a beach. Her supple body was barely covered by the small two-piece she was wearing. Her hair was wet from the ocean and grains of sand clung to her tan as she stared provocatively into the camera, posing with the skill and poise of a Sports Illustrated model.

Chris zoomed in on the photograph and gazed at it for a long time. He felt his pants grow tighter. Michelle was on the other side of the house and he paused for a moment, trying to weigh up the chances of her walking in on him. He looked again at the photograph of Elize on the beach. Then, in one swift movement, he pushed his chair back, stepped across to close the study door, and returned to his position in front of the computer.

The week had passed quickly and Rachel was busy mopping the tiles in the main entrance when she heard the buzzer for the intercom to the front gate. She ignored the sound and continued mopping, assuming that it was one of the beggars who would often ring during the day asking for a 'piece job' or charity. The buzzer rang once more, this time more persistently, and Rachel placed the mop in the water bucket. She wiped the sweat from her forehead and picked up the receiver.

'Hello.'

'Hello, Rachel? It's Karlien here. Michelle's friend?'

'Mrs Jordaan isn't here. She went out with Mrs Am -'

'Oh, I know,' Karlien said over the crackling intercom, cutting Rachel off mid-sentence. 'We wanted to get her out of the house so that we could set up a surprise for her. Can you open up and let us in?'

Rachel paused for a moment as she tried to think whether she was allowed to let them in, knowing that she didn't really have a choice in the matter. She pushed the button on the intercom that opened the front gate and moved the mop out the way so that she could open the security gate to let the visitors in. She looked up the driveway and watched as several cars drove in, expensive vehicles that shone in the mid-morning sunlight. Car doors opened and well-dressed women emerged from them, greeting each other through designer sunglasses and with whitened smiles. They carried an array of things: trays of finger-snacks, bottles of wine and a variety of pastel gift bags.

Rachel stepped forward to greet Karlien, who was trying to juggle a tray of sausage rolls and lock her car at the same time. She and Karlien had met occasionally but had rarely spent any time in each others' company. She liked her, though, this woman with glossy dark hair and fair skin. She had sent Rachel a bouquet of flowers when she heard about Maia. The next time she'd come to the house to see Michelle, she had taken the time to ask Rachel how she was doing. She seemed like a nice woman, even from behind the line that separated them.

'*Ag*, thanks, Rachel. It's good to see you.' Karlien was taking strain, trying to negotiate the uneven steps in her very high heels. 'We have about an hour to set this all up. Do you think you could give us a hand?'

Rachel nodded. She grabbed the tray of sausage rolls so that Karlien wouldn't break her neck. The other women followed, murmuring greetings with averted eyes as they walked past Rachel and into the house. Rachel had got used to this. They were all speaking to each other in rapid Afrikaans, a gust of words that flew clean over her head. They obviously all knew what had happened and were trying their best to be respectful of her while still enjoying themselves.

In the lounge some of Michelle's friends were arranging presents and erecting a giant 'IT'S A ???' banner over the fireplace. The others were in the kitchen, taking clingwrap off platters and opening cupboards to find glasses.

The lounge was almost ready when Karlien received a text message on her smartphone and she held up her hand. 'Shhhh,' she said. A couple of the women suppressing squeals, the friends all stopped what they were doing and started darting around the room. Rachel looked on, confused. Then she realised that for some reason they were all looking for places to hide. They scrambled behind couches and cabinets, their outfits and heels not making it easy.

Rachel went into one of the adjacent rooms and stayed there, where she could still see what was going on in the lounge. She heard keys moving in the front gate and watched as the door opened to reveal a blindfolded Michelle being led into the house by her friend Chantelle, who had a big smile on her face.

'Almost there,' Chantelle said as she guided Michelle through the house towards the lounge. 'Mind the step.'

Chantelle positioned Michelle in the middle of the room and paused for a moment in an attempt to build the suspense.

'Okay. Take it off now,' she said.

Michelle did as she was instructed. She pulled off the blindfold and blinked around the room. She looked dazed. At that precise moment all her friends jumped out from their hiding places, throwing streamers and confetti over her.

'SURPRISE!'

Michelle started to laugh. 'What on – What are you *doing*?' she said, squinting her eyes and putting her arms over her head as confetti rained down on her.

'It's your baby shower!' Karlien said. She stepped forward and placed a crown on Michelle's head that read 'Mom of the Year'.

Then Chantelle grabbed Michelle by the hand and led her towards the couch in the middle of the festivities. Michelle laughed as she greeted her friends individually, and gradually the noise levels in the room reached something like fever pitch. They exchanged jokes and pastries, everyone talking over each other with infectious enthusiasm, all of them wanting to get a chance to talk to their friend who had insisted on being so reclusive for most of her pregnancy.

Rachel, coming into the lounge with the warmed up sausage rolls, flinched when she heard her name mentioned in the flood of Afrikaans. She saw Michelle look up at her, noticing her presence for the first time. Karlien took the tray from her hands and said, 'I was just telling Michelle how you let us in and helped set everything up.'

'*Dankie*, Rachel,' Michelle said. 'I appreciate it.'

The women excitedly started to hand Michelle her gifts, urging her to open them so that they could witness her reactions. Rachel retreated to the kitchen, their laughter growing softer as she left the room. She walked over to the counter and leaned against it, closing her eyes and exhaling as she tried to control her feelings. She heard footsteps from behind and inhaled deeply. By the time she turned around her face was a mask.

'Oh, there you are.' It was Karlien, peeking around the door. 'It's time for us to have the cake. Can you help me bring it out?'

Rachel nodded. She walked over to the large red velvet cake

that was on the table. The words 'Say Goodbye To Your Sleep' were written on the white icing in chocolate sauce. Karlien took one side while Rachel took the other and together they walked with great care through to the lounge, Karlien's high heels clicking on the tiles as they made their way.

'Time for cake!' Karlien said excitedly, navigating towards the table while the others made room for it. 'Do any of you know if we're meant to sing anything?'

Everyone laughed and clapped their hands as Karlien and Rachel lowered the cake to the surface.

'This looks incredible,' Chantelle said, picking up a knife and handing it to Michelle. 'Where did you get it, Karlien?'

'Bianca made it,' Karlien said, pointing to a blonde woman who was sitting to the side on one of the dining room chairs. 'Glutton free.'

'Gluten free,' Bianca corrected.

Karlien winked. 'Isn't that what I said?'

They all laughed and excited chatter broke out again, most of it in Afrikaans.

Feeling more intruder than participant in the moment, Rachel stepped back. She was about to leave the room when Karlien motioned for her by clicking her fingers in the air.

'*Ag*, Rachel,' she called in English, 'can you just help us clear these cups and plates? It'll give us some room to serve the cake.'

'No, it's fine, Karlien,' Michelle said, placing a hand on her friend's knee. 'Let Rachel – '

'Don't be silly,' Karlien said. 'There's no room here and it'll only take her a few seconds.'

Karlien began to scrape and stack the dirty cups and cutlery, piling them onto Rachel's outheld arms until she was balancing a large mass of porcelain almost up to her chin. She left the lounge and made her way towards the kitchen, her back straight and her breathing steadier than her heart. Standing in the empty kitchen, she listened to the women's voices. They had reverted to Afrikaans again and as they spoke, the foreign words making the difference between her world and theirs even starker, she was filled with an all-consuming anger.

Rachel stood dead still, waiting for the emotion to pass, but her arms under the heavy load were shaking. The dirty cups and plates began to rattle. When a shriek of laughter came from the lounge something inside of her snapped. Lifting her arms to increase the momentum, with one fierce, vicious movement Rachel jerked them apart and all the dishes, as well as a few wineglasses that were in the crossfire on the counter top close by, crashed to the tiled floor. The glass and porcelain shattered upon impact, while pieces of the heavier crockery bounced before breaking and shot to all corners of the kitchen. In the hush that followed, the only sound coming from one stubborn saucer spinning and slowly clunking to a stop, Rachel allowed her arms to fall to her sides. She heard cries of fright and then high-pitched voices coming from the lounge. Rachel stayed where she was, not moving, although her heart was pounding. She took a few more seconds to savour the moment before kneeling down on the tiles. She began to gather up some of the larger broken pieces. She heard high heels hurry into the kitchen and then stop.

'What on earth happened?' Karlien asked, her eyes wide.

'They slipped,' said Rachel. She kept her eyes on her task.

Karlien took in the damage. The kitchen floor was strewn from one end to the other in broken pieces of glass and porcelain.

'You almost gave us a heart attack!'

'I'm sorry,' Rachel said.

'Are you hurt?'

Rachel shook her head and Karlien, taking in the carnage one last time, left the kitchen to report back to the others. Rachel sat back on her heels, waiting and listening. No one else was coming to survey the scene of disaster, it seemed. Not Michelle either. The adrenalin was slowly seeping away. As she listened to the sound of the women resuming their festivities, although more muted now, she marvelled at what she had just done and how easily she had gotten away with it. She felt empowered, as though she could move through the house and do the same to every item the Jordaans owned.

She fetched the dustpan and brush from the broom cupboard and started to sweep everything into one central pile, satisfaction moving steadily through her.

She felt stronger.

Michelle was putting on her heels when Chris walked into the bedroom, holding up a red tie and a black one against his shirt for her to comment on. They were going to a stage production at the Montecasino Teatro and the event called for 'smart casual' attire.

'Black,' Michelle said as she struggled to get her foot into the shoe. The weight she'd put on during this pregnancy had made her a whole shoe-size larger than she'd been when she'd bought these heels. If she could have had it her way, she'd have gone to the theatre in tracksuit and slippers but she knew this wasn't really an option.

Exhausted from the effort it took to jam her feet into the shoes,

Michelle sat back on the bed and looked up at Chris unenthusiastically.

'Do we have to go?' she asked, not for the first time.

'You're the one who bought the tickets,' Chris pointed out, talking to his reflection in the mirror as he assessed his outfit. 'Which reminds me: did you print them out yet?'

'No, they're still on my laptop,' Michelle answered. She sat up. 'Can you do it, Chris?'

After he left the bedroom Michelle got up and moved to the dressing table. She began to apply her make-up. She grew less attractive with each month that passed, she decided as she stared at her reflection and the bloated version of the woman she used to be stared sullenly back at her.

'I booked it about three months ago,' Michelle called out in an attempt to help Chris find the tickets. 'Search for Marie ...'

There was no response and she continued applying her make-up, the transformative effect of red lipstick and mascara making her a little more confident about her appearance. She brushed her hair, then got up to go and see what was keeping Chris.

He was standing in the doorway, her laptop in his hand.

'What is this shit?' he asked in a tone she'd never heard her husband use before.

Confused, Michelle approached him. She looked at the screen, trying to see what he was talking about, what had upset him so much that he was literally shaking with emotion.

It was the email response from the women's clinic.

'Oh, that ... it's nothing...' she began. 'Chris – '

'The fuck it's nothing.'

'That email was from three months ago,' Michelle said. 'I was in a strange place and I just wanted to …'

'Kill our fucking baby? After all we went through to fall pregnant?'

'No, that's not what – Chris, please, it was just a query.'

'To an *abortion* clinic, Michelle! Do you have any idea how messed up that is?'

'I was confused …'

'That's why you didn't want to find out the sex of the baby, wasn't it?'

'No – but –'

'It's my child too.'

This last statement hit its mark. The desire to remain calm and be rational was instantly replaced by Michelle's default position: the need to fight back.

'*Your* child?! But I'm the one who has to carry *your* child!' she shouted, tears causing her freshly applied mascara to run down her cheeks. '*I'm* the one who had to give up my job! *I'm* the one who had to change everything and sit here all day while you spend your time flirting with that … that … *slut*, whoever she is!'

Chris stared back at her, impassive.

'Oh, you don't think I know?' Michelle was still on the attack. 'You don't think I saw all the little comments on Facebook?'

'Do you blame me?' Chris replied calmly. 'The last time you and I had sex, Michelle, was when we made that baby, the one you want to kill. Guess it's just another child to add to your list.'

Chris's words cut through like knives, piercing straight through to the hurt and guilt that had been growing like a tumour inside her ever since ... ever since ...

'It wasn't my fault.' Michelle still felt the need to defend herself.

'No? Whose fault was it then? Who was it who was meant to be looking after Maia that day? Me? Rachel? Richmond? No, Michelle, it was you! Maia was *your* responsibility! Yours alone.'

'I told you I was busy!' Michelle screamed back, trying to block his words out.

'A five-year-old girl died because you were "busy", Michelle.'

Michelle lashed at Chris then, her hand flying through the air towards his face, but he caught her wrist in mid-air. He held it tightly and then, controlling her hand like a puppet master, used it to slap himself in the face, striking himself methodically, over and over again until he was satisfied that he had proven his point. Michelle's palm stung from the force with which he struck himself but she refused to acknowledge the pain. She glared at her husband. Her eyes were dry now but she had gone very pale. Chris held her hand against his chest for a second and then slowly forced it to travel down his stomach towards his belt line, his eyes not leaving Michelle's. He didn't blink or look away from her face and the pain in his eyes was raw. He waited for her hand to reach his crotch before he let it go, tossing it to the side contemptuously.

'Guess what?' Chris said, snapping the laptop shut and putting it on the dressing table. 'That's the first time you've tried to touch me in months.'

Michelle massaged her wrist and said nothing as she watched Chris walk out of their bedroom. A minute later she heard the jangle of keys and the slam of the front door.

Chris rolled down the windows of the Z4 as he drove onto the N3 highway, the night wind beating against his face as the car picked up speed. He didn't care where he was heading as long as it took him away from the house. Music blared through his sound system, aggressive rock music with dark tones that complemented his emotion. The anger was on him like a second layer of skin, a tangible presence that clung to his body. It made him want to scratch at it, claw at the anger until his arms bled, like Michelle had wanted to claw at his face.

He pushed his foot down on the accelerator and watched as the dial rose from 120km to 140km, the engine roaring as the car sped along the highway. He opened his mouth and screamed out loud, his frustration swallowed up by the wind that rushed through the windows and tugged at his hair. He put his hand on the horn and pressed hard, holding it there while the harsh, ugly sound blared into the night. He beat the horn with his palm, and kept beating it until the rage started to subside.

He was about 10km into his journey to nowhere when a light came on on the dashboard, indicating that he was close to running on empty. Taking the off-ramp to the closest petrol station he knew of, Chris pulled in and filled up his tank. While he waited for the attendant to clean his windscreen and his breathing steadied, he took out his phone and opened his Facebook account. It was reflex more than intention. He noted that Anja had just checked into a nightclub called Movida, the address telling him that it was only a few blocks away from where he was.

Chris paid for the petrol and prepared to drive back out onto the road. He stopped at the T-junction. Right would take him home; left would take him in the direction of the club. He looked down at the phone on his lap. There was a photo of Anja on the dance floor with her friends, a drink in her hand, smiling for the camera.

'Fuck it,' Chris muttered to himself and took a left, using the Google Maps app to help orientate himself. He was at the club in less than fifteen minutes. He turned into the parking lot and, after tossing a piece of gum into his mouth, climbed out of the car and walked briskly towards the red carpet that led to the entrance. He paid the entrance fee and the bouncer stamped his wrist with a large 'M' before stepping aside so that he could enter.

Chris hadn't been in a club for well over a decade but, from the look of things, nothing had changed. He scanned the dark venue for Anja, the Moulin Rouge-themed decor glittering red and gold and the music thumping around him. He was about to move to the second dance floor when he saw her standing at the bar. She was wearing a black cocktail dress and laughing as she took a shot of something. The blonde girl from her Facebook photos was standing beside her.

Breathing in, Chris approached the bar and watched as Anja's eyes grew wide when she recognised him. She beckoned for him to join them and, wrapping her arms around him, greeted him with a kiss on the cheek.

'What on earth are *you* doing here?' she shouted over the noise, standing close to him so that she could be heard. 'It's a school night!'

'I could say the same thing,' Chris shouted in response.

Anja stepped back and gave him one of her big, lovely smiles, then took him by the hand so that she could introduce him to her friend.

'Elize! This is my boss!'

Elize was even prettier in person. She extended her hand and gave Chris a slightly lopsided smile. Her eyes were heavy from alcohol.

'Hello, boss,' she drawled.

Chris took the hand Elize held out to him and smiled back, looking over his shoulder for Anja, who burst out laughing. She put her hand on Chris's shoulder and touched her mouth to his ear.

'I guess I'm going to have to behave myself now ... boss.'

'Oh, don't let me spoil your evening – and I'm not your boss,' Chris said. He looked around the club casually as though he were searching for somebody. 'I'm actually here to meet up with a friend for his birthday but I can't see him anywhere.'

'Well, that just means you'll have to have a drink with us until he gets here.'

'Guess the first round is on me then.'

'Music to my ears,' Elize butted in, putting her hand on his shoulder too.

Chris shook his head and laughed. 'What are you ladies drinking?' he asked

'Tequila!' they both chimed.

It was well past midnight and Rachel was still awake. Shouting coming from the house earlier had told her that all was not well with the Jordaans. She had heard the sound of Chris's car leaving the property and the Z4's tyres screeching in the road as he drove off. Sleepless as usual, she hadn't heard him return yet.

She reached under her pillow and pulled out the stolen ultrasound, staring at the outline of the baby in the moonlight that came from the window. While she had nothing against the baby itself, she hated everything that this fuzzy grey outline represented. In it was all the loss that she had suffered in her time here at the

Jordaans. Channelling her pain into the ultrasound had become a nightly ritual for her. It had gradually replaced prayers and scripture, time that Rachel now used to will her hatred out from herself and direct it towards Michelle.

As Rachel found herself drifting towards sleep, the ultrasound on her chest, suddenly the ghastly screaming cry of the pool cleaner brought her to an instant sitting position and she was back: back to the day when her world had fallen apart. It was a sound she would never forget because she had heard it moments before – In fact it had been the screams of the pool cleaner that had drawn her to the garden, as though that soulless machine had been calling to her, warning her that her life was about to be shattered forever.

Shaking, she lay back down again, but her heart was racing. The sound was relentless, unearthly. It shrieked and sobbed and screamed, begging to be released from wherever it was stuck. As it began to choke and gasp, Rachel felt the tears begin to flow. She turned onto her stomach and pulled the pillow over her head.

Michelle woke with a start. The space where Chris usually slept was empty but the static from their argument still felt tangible in the air. The wretched pool cleaner was stuck again. Even though Chris had identified the sound for her, and she knew that the machine was just struggling to return to the depths of the pool, she still found it impossible to ignore. She tried to block it out but the screaming was too much.

Climbing awkwardly out of bed, Michelle walked through the empty house and, after deactivating the alarm, made her way to the kitchen door. The cold grass burned her warm feet as she walked across the lawn towards the swimming pool, the light from the house casting harsh shadows that made it difficult for her to see where she was going.

The shrieks grew louder. They were coming from the corner closest to her. Michelle bent over and yanked the cleaner out of the water, the hard plastic head struggling like a live thing in her hands. She screamed at the machine in frustration and ripped the head from the pipes. Then she hurled the whole contraption to the ground as hard as she could.

Unattached, the lengths of tubing slithered back into the water. The garden fell into an uneasy silence. Exhausted and sopping wet, Michelle strode over to the decapitated head and threw it back into the pool. She stood and watched it sink to the dark bottom beneath the deep green layer of scum.

Wiping her forehead, she peered into the filthy water for a few minutes. Then, decisively, she walked over to the shed that housed the water pump and opened the wooden door. There was a very large bottle of chlorine inside and she picked it up and took it back to the edge of the swimming pool. She unscrewed the lid and was hit by a pungent, almost overpowering chemical smell. Holding the open container at arm's length over the surface of the pool, she began to dispense the chlorine, casting the white powder like snowflakes in wide arcs. Where one cup would have sufficed, Michelle kept pouring until her arm ached and the container was empty. She watched as the chlorine dissolved into the murky water. Then she threw the container into the pool.

Standing alone in the dark garden, her arms at her sides, Michelle waited for the normal nighttime sounds of the suburbs to return now that the cries of the pool cleaner had gone. Now, however, that desolate noise was replaced by something else, something deep inside her head, a sound that no chemical could erase.

'This has to end,' she murmured. 'This has to end.'

chapter 20

RACHEL CLIMBED INTO Chris's BMW. The carriage was lower than any vehicle she had ever driven in. She settled into the black leather seat and looked around for the seatbelt while she waited for Chris to get in the driver's side. The car was beautiful, without a doubt, but as Rachel looked over her shoulder she saw that there was very little room for anything other than two passengers and possibly a few additional items. There was no room for a baby, let alone a pushchair or a car seat. Rachel wondered if Chris would sell the car if he and Michelle ever had children.

The engine and the aircon roared to life at the same time as the sound system filled the car with the music from Jacaranda FM, the local radio station Chris must listen to when his smartphone wasn't plugged in. Rachel held her papers and handbag rigidly on her lap and smiled at Chris as he closed the door and started to reverse up the driveway.

As they backed into the street Rachel saw Maria standing on the pavement outside the house where she worked. A huge smile spread across her face when she recognised Rachel in the passenger seat. Maria started to laugh and flick her finger in the air, an action which caused Rachel to smile and shake her head. She didn't want to draw Chris's attention to her friend's behaviour, but he had already noticed.

'Why's she doing that?' Chris asked, waving at Maria as they drove past.

'She's teasing me.'

'Why?'

'Well, it's not every day that I get a ride in a car like this to the taxi rank,' Rachel replied, looking shyly down at her papers.

Chris laughed as he turned down the street, the car slowing down to a painful pace as it joined the rest of the morning traffic. Rachel watched Chris glance in the rearview mirror, his fingers drumming to the beat of the music on the radio, then reach up to the mirror and adjust it. Rachel sat in silence, unsure how to communicate with her employer in this context.

'So how long do they give you on the visa?' Chris asked.

Perhaps he was trying to dilute the awkward silence and for that she was grateful.

'Six months,' Rachel answered, even though she knew he knew that information already.

'I heard they're cracking down on the illegals who jump the fence.'

'It's getting difficult to be here if you don't have a visa.'

'Good thing you've got one then.' Chris inched the car forward.

'Yes, your letter helped me a lot.'

'How are things in Mozambique now? It hasn't been in the news for a while.'

'They are okay,' Rachel replied, talking to her papers. 'My mother and father say that it's getting better.'

'Where are you from again?' Chris asked. 'Something with an 'I', isn't it?'

'Inhassoro,' Rachel said.

'Oh yes, Inhassoro,' Chris said. 'I've heard there are some great diving spots out there. I had a friend who went on holiday to Mozambique a few years ago and he couldn't stop talking about how nice it was. Especially all the cheap seafood.'

'It is a beautiful place,' Rachel murmured.

They fell into silence until they were near the taxi rank.

'You can just drop me here, Chris,' Rachel said.

'Don't be silly. I'll take you right in.'

Chris nosed the BMW through the taxi rank area, negotiating carefully around the beat-up vehicles and coming to a stop close to the exit. Rachel discovered that she had slid quite far down into her seat. The expensive car drew more than its fair share of attention and, as Rachel opened the car door, she could sense the collective eyes of the passengers and taxi drivers all over her. This was one of the reasons why she had not wanted Chris to take her to the taxi rank in the first place, let alone right inside, but to try and explain it to him would have been a waste of breath.

'Thank you for the ride,' she said.

'Anytime.' Chris replied. 'Anytime.'

With that, Rachel closed the door and Chris drove off with an embarrassing burst of speed and music. She walked without looking back towards the taxis that were going in her direction. The taxi rank was an open space of tarred chaos, filled with people and vehicles coming and going to different parts of the city and its environs. There was the occasional vendor but for the most part they were outside, up on the road; this was a space filled with litter and busy commuters. With no shade or trees to protect them from the morning sun, the place was already boiling hot and Rachel was forced to stop and take off her jersey before carrying on.

She did her best to ignore the stares and rude comments that were coming from the people around her but one driver, a short Zulu man, seemed hellbent on making sure she didn't miss out on what he had to say to her. Running up alongside Rachel and matching his pace to hers, he put his arm around her waist and walked with her as though they were a couple. His breath stank of old cigarettes and cheap whiskey.

'Hey, sweetie. What do you have to do to get a ride in such a nice car?' he asked.

Rachel ignored him and walked faster, a response that just caused the driver to laugh and step up his pace. He put his arm around her shoulder and sniffed her neck, leering as he smelled her. Rachel shrugged her shoulders forcefully in an attempt to get him to let go of her and as soon as she was free from his embrace, she walked as fast as she could to put distance between them. The driver stood still and watched her leave, sucking his browning teeth before spitting on the dirt.

'Fuckin' makwerekwere bitch,' he said, grabbing his crotch to prove a point. 'They suck on anything to get ahead.'

Rachel ignored the racial slur that local South Africans used for foreigners and soon she had disappeared into the crowd of people. She pushed her way to the front of the line so that she could get a seat on the taxi. When most people thought of racism in South Africa they usually simplified it to black versus white or European versus African, she knew, but it was so much more layered than that. During her time in South Africa Rachel had found that the attitude of local black people towards those who came from some other countries in Africa was much more aggressive than white people's.

For the most part white and black still lived very separate lives here. For black people, things were different. Many South African blacks were forced by circumstance to live alongside the foreign ones, in townships or other densely populated informal settlements. Sometimes this proximity resulted in xenophobia, and attacks against the descendants of Zimbabwe, Mozambique, Malawi and Nigeria were not uncommon. The locals felt that the foreigners were stealing their jobs, their women and their land and, with unemployment statistics on the rise, they felt that it was their duty to protect what Mandela had given them by using the very tactics that he had stood against in the later part of his political career.

South Africa was a melting pot of cultures. The pot could explode at any time. It just needed the slightest of sparks. Rachel dreaded the day she herself might be caught in the crossfire of a xenophobic attack. This was why she chose not to talk too much at taxi ranks and marketplaces, knowing that her foreign accent automatically placed her in a potentially dangerous position.

She climbed into the taxi and took a seat by the window where, holding tightly to her paperwork and passport, she waited for fifteen other passengers to board the vehicle. The taxi roared to life and the radio began to crackle with loud kwaito music. Frantic township rhythms throbbed through the vehicle. Rachel closed her eyes and held onto the window as the minibus left the taxi rank and sped into the traffic, the driver honking on the horn as he tried to move past cars and take gaps wherever they presented themselves – and even when they didn't.

Rachel rocked back and forth with the rhythm of the taxi, trying not to drop her bag and papers. She hoped Maia was behaving herself with Michelle. The last thing she needed was to get back and find out that she had broken one of Michelle's expensive vases or knocked over one of the sculptures that were positioned around the house. Maia was getting a little too comfortable with speaking her mind amongst adults, too, a bad habit she'd picked up from the other children at school, and Rachel was struggling to figure out the best way of dealing with this. If they were in Mozambique, the attitude would have been smacked out of her but here in Johannesburg it looked as though she would need to employ a different method to correct her child.

Just don't spill anything on the white carpet, Maia.

chapter 21

MICHELLE FLIPPED THROUGH the classifieds in the newspaper, the fresh pages crinkling as she went. It was just before 7am and, unable to sleep, she had gone through to the study to pass the time until Rachel started her day. She hoped Chris would arrive home before he had to be at work so that he could at least shower and have something to eat.

Her tea had gone cold on the table beside her. She scanned past the sections advertising property and second-hand goods until she found the Jobs section, which took up almost half of the page. Picking up a red marker, she started to read the small paragraphs that marketed the services of gardeners and domestic workers, stating their qualities and what services they were able to provide prospective employers.

She had found Rachel by doing a similar search all those years back and had learned quickly how to discern which applicant best suited what she was looking for. One thing she had learned from her experience with Rachel was to ascertain whether the applicant was pregnant or planning on starting a family. Had Rachel told them up front that she was expecting Maia, they probably wouldn't have hired her and, when she revealed it to them, it was too late to look for another maid. Legally, they would have been obliged to give her maternity leave anyway, which would have meant that, for four months, they would have had to have a second domestic worker come in on a casual basis to do the work that Rachel had been hired to do. Even though Michelle respected and understood that this was a given for any employer/employee relationship, she was well aware that Rachel had taken advantage of them by keeping her pregnancy secret when she had applied for the job. She hadn't really resented it then, but she did now. What could have ended up being a poor start to their working relationship had been alleviated by the fact that both she and Chris had believed sincerely that this was an opportunity to provide security and support to someone who needed it the most. They had been reading a lot about social upliftment during that time and saw it as a chance to 'give back'.

Michelle circled a couple of names, noting that just about all the ads were from people from Malawi or Zimbabwe. Most of her friends employed foreign gardeners and domestic workers and were perfectly up front about their motives: because they worked harder, they claimed, than local workers, and for a lot less money. The locals had an air of entitlement about them and were more likely to take their employers to the labour court if they were fired, whereas foreigners were grateful for the work and would do their best to please their employers because their visas and families back home depended on them. Michelle recognised that in many ways she was taking advantage of the unfortunate situation this workforce found themselves in but she also believed that a low-paying job was better than no job and so was happy to give the job to someone who was willing to take it over someone who would end up being lazy and entitled.

Michelle heard the front door open. She looked up from the paper. Chris was about to walk past the study but took a step back when he saw her sitting there. He was wearing the same clothes he had worn the night before and his face was covered in stubble.

'Are you ready?' Chris asked, acting as if nothing had happened between them the night before and that it wasn't unusual for him to stay out all night.

'For what?'

'Your appointment.'

Michelle put the lid on the marker. To be honest, she was surprised that, after all that had happened and the terrible fight they had had last night, Chris still *wanted* to go with her to her appointment with Dr Pieterse. He looked as though he had slept in the car but she chose not to say anything about his appearance. A snide comment right now would do more harm than good.

'Almost,' she said.

'I'm going to go change my shirt and then we can go.'

Michelle folded the newspaper and left it on her desk, then followed Chris down the passage to their bedroom to freshen up.

Rachel had just finished her morning bath when she heard the electronic gate open and the Z4 reverse up the driveway. She took her time getting ready for the day. First she returned the ultrasound photograph to the red biscuit tin. Then she put on her uniform, bent to look in the mirror, and adjusted the collar and belt.

The first signs of spring had finally started to appear. She looked forward to walking down the path from her room to the Jordaans' house in the morning sun instead of the dark cold.

The coffee machine was already on from Chris's morning fix and, knowing that Michelle no longer drank it, Rachel turned it off so that she could clean it. It didn't sound like Michelle was awake yet and so, once she had finished stacking the dishwasher, she walked through the house to assess the damage that awaited her in the other rooms.

Were this her own house, Rachel would have had family members in every room, and not necessarily by choice. One of the things she had never understood about the culture here in the suburbs was the way that families lived apart from each other, even if it was only a few streets away. In Inhassoro, families lived on the same property, raised their children together and shared the costs of living. And while it could sometimes get very crowded, back home she could never say she had ever spent a night in loneliness.

It was as though need brought people together, and plenty split them apart.

As she walked past Michelle's study she spotted a half-full mug on her desk and went into the room to collect it. She was about to leave when she noticed the newspaper. She picked it up, intending to see if there was anything worth reading with her mid-morning tea. As she scanned through the pages her attention was drawn to some blots of red bleeding through the newsprint and she navigated her way towards the marked page.

Rachel stared at the red circles. They had been drawn around the names of four women looking for domestic work. She lowered the paper in shock, trying to process what she had just discovered.

The Jordaans were planning to replace her.

Suddenly the telephone in the study started to ring, its shrill voice startling Rachel. Hastily she folded the newspaper and put it back on Michelle's desk. She cleared her throat and picked up the receiver.

'You're through to the Jordaans' house, Rachel speaking, how may I help you?'

'Rachel, it's me.'

The sound of her mother's voice brought with it a sense of comfort, even as it mixed with dread as she anticipated the bad news that would have prompted her mother to call her on the Jordaans' landline.

'What's wrong?' she asked.

'Your father is sick, my girl. We need money for medicine.'

'What's wrong with him?'

'He has had a chest cold for many weeks. The doctor says it might be TB.'

'How much do you need?'

'Five thousand meticais.'

Rachel gasped before she could stop herself.

'I don't have that much, Mama.'

'Can't you borrow from your boss? I'm sure they would understand.'

Rachel looked over at the folded newspaper, the red stains from the marker pen still visible. The Jordaans would not understand; in fact they were the last people she could turn to for help right now.

'I'll find a way to get it, Mama,' Rachel said.

She hung up the phone and hurried to the front door. She ran up the path to her room, got down on her knees and and pulled the biscuit tin out from under the bed. At the wooden table, she popped the lid open and took out all the cash that was in there, first counting out the meticais and then the South African money, most of it what she had managed to save over the last few months, and a few notes from Michelle's purse. She counted R500 and just under MZN1 000.

It wasn't enough. Not even close.

She replaced the money in the tin and pushed it under the bed with her toe. Then she locked her door and went back to the house. In the kitchen she paced back and forth like an animal testing the perimeters of its cage. She needed to find the money quickly but there was absolutely no way she could ask Chris or Michelle for it. She hadn't even been able yet to process the fact that they were looking for another maid and that she would shortly be out of a job. The urgency of her father's situation had moved to the forefront of her mind and was demanding all of her attention.

As she paced back and forth past the window that overlooked the garden, she noticed the heavy rug she had asked Richmond a few days ago to hang out on the washing line to air. Chris kept an old tennis racket in the broom cupboard beside the fridge. He used it for hitting tennis balls around the garden for Hugo to chase. She took it out and marched straight over to the rug and began beating it as hard as she could. Clouds of dust rose with every stroke. Rachel struck the rug again, harder and harder, until she was thrashing wildly at the lifeless thing, beating it with all her strength, tears of anger soon mixing with the dirt that was flying around her.

Hitting it one last time, she let out a scream of sheer frustration. Then she flung the racket onto the grass and dropped to her knees, feeling all the fight drain out of her. Out of breath and with a now throbbing headache, she lay crying on the grass, sobbing into her arms.

Michelle sat back while Dr Pieterse carried out her examination. Chris was seated a few feet away, watching the image on the monitor. The baby moved as it responded to the pressure from the doctor's hand and Michelle shifted her position to compensate. There was no doubting that there was a human on the screen; the detail in its fingers and toes was remarkably clear. Satisfied with what she had seen, Dr Pieterse smiled at them.

'I'm happy to see that your blood pressure has returned to normal, Michelle,' she said.

Chris and Michelle smiled back, glad that they had the doctor's approval.

'Heartbeat's strong, the placenta is in a good position and your baby is growing steadily, following a nice curve. Are we still happy to go the caesarean route?'

Michelle nodded and Dr Pieterse checked a box on her notepad.

'And the sex? Have you decided whether you want to know?'

'We want it to be a surprise,' Chris answered, not looking at Michelle.

'All right then.' Dr Pieterse put the notepad on a side table and took off her reading glasses. 'Well, all that's left for us to do now is decide what date you'd like your baby's birthday to be.'

'How much can I get for this?' Rachel asked, pushing the diamond ring across the glass counter towards the man in the Cash Converters store. 'It's four carats.'

She watched as the balding white man held the piece of jewellery up so that he could examine it in the light, clearly not as enamoured with it as Rachel had been when she'd found it on the beach all those years ago.

'Five t'ousand,' the man said in a thick Mediterranean accent. 'You won't get better anywhere else.'

Rachel had expected the ring to fetch at least R7 000. She wondered whether it was worth trying to negotiate with him. The problem was that men like this could sense the desperation on the people who walked through their doors. They knew they carried all the power in the situation. She slid her cellphone across the counter.

'And now?'

The Cash Converters man smiled condescendingly. It was an old cellphone and they both knew it.

'Five t'ousand five hun'red,' he said.

Rachel nodded.

In one practised movement the man scooped up both items. He disappeared into a room at the back of the store and returned a few minutes later with a wad of notes, which he counted out until Rachel had a small pile in front of her. She waited. The man raised an eyebrow.

'Can I have an envelope, please?' Rachel asked.

He looked at her and sighed. Then, as though he were doing her the biggest favour in the world, he reached under the cash-till and pulled out a grubby brown envelope. He put the money inside it and handed it to her, at the same time looking over her shoulder at two young men who had entered the store with a sound system. His eyes flickered impatiently towards Rachel. He gestured for her to move aside.

Rachel turned to one side and slid the envelope inside her bra. As she left the store she glanced around to see if anyone was following her. It was well known that petty thieves would identify people as they left pawnshops and rob them of the cash they had just collected in exchange for their goods. Satisfied that she wasn't being followed, she made her way back to the taxi rank where she waited for a ride to her side of town.

She had enough money for the emergency back home now and she felt a sense of relief. She would send it to her parents that afternoon.

Chris swung his racket with all his might, sending the black rubber ball hurtling across the squash court into the wall, where it bounced back towards Hannes, who returned with a shot of equal vigour. They were in the middle of an intense rally and Chris was down, with Hannes needing two more points to win the game. Chris swung again, narrowly missing the ball.

Match point.

Hannes served and Chris returned the shot. He swung wildly as he prepared himself for the return. Hannes ran forward and lightly tapped the ball, causing it to fall short of the area where Chris had been expecting it to land. He ran forward and lunged for the ball but it was already on its second bounce before he could get to it. Unable to check his momentum in time, he slammed into the wall, his shoulder taking the full force of the impact. Cursing, Chris threw his racket to the ground. His lungs were burning. He bent over and put his hands on his knees as he tried to catch his breath, sweat pouring from his forehead.

After a couple of minutes, he straightened up and walked over to Hannes. They shook hands and Chris patted his friend on the back to congratulate him on his win. Usually on the occasions that he beat Chris, Hannes would gloat jokingly but today he held back. Puzzled, still breathing hard after his exertions, Chris headed to the glass door at the back of the court but Hannes didn't follow him.

Chris turned his head and looked at him enquiringly.

'What was that about?' Hannes asked, wiping his face on his towel.

Chris didn't answer. He picked up his water bottle where he'd left it beside the door and sat down on the wooden floor with his back against the wall.

'Home?' Hannes asked. He sat on the floor beside Chris.

'Yeah,' Chris replied, taking a sip of water and staring straight ahead. 'I feel like I'm living in a cemetery.'

'How so?'

'Michelle gets colder every day. Rachel is like a walking corpse.'

'Are they fighting with each other?'

'No.' Chris sighed. 'I'd prefer that, to be honest. They're doing this passive aggressive thing of not talking to each other, which makes it really difficult for Michelle to rest. It stresses her out. And when I get home I have to listen to her bitch about it. With the way things are, I'd prefer to stay later at work than go home and listen to all of that.'

'Hmm,' Hannes murmured. 'I heard you went out with Anja on Thursday.'

Chris nodded.

'Watch out for that.'

Chris nodded again, still staring at the space in front of him. Hannes said nothing further to fill the silence. Hannes was right, Chris knew and, if he was honest, he was grateful that someone else was keeping an eye on his life, even if it was his not very articulate friend from the office.

'I'm here if you need to talk,' Hannes added awkwardly. He held his fist up for Chris to bump and Chris did.

'Thanks, man, appreciate it.'

'You should probably talk to someone else about your game, though. You were shit today,' Hannes said. He gave Chris a light smack on the side of his head and began to struggle to his feet.

Chris shook his head and chuckled. He gave his water bottle a squeeze and sent its contents splattering into Hannes's red sweaty face. 'Chop,' he said.

Michelle had spent most of the morning alone, with Rachel being out for the day renewing her visa at Home Affairs. She decided to restore some order to her study and, while straightening the books on the bookshelf, she came across Chris's digital camera. It had been an expensive gadget, bought when Chris had fancied himself as something of a photographer.

Turning it on, Michelle was surprised to see that there was still some life in the battery. The flashing icon indicated that it had 30 minutes of power left. Michelle navigated her way through the menu until she found the photo gallery and started going through the memory card to see what she and Chris had stored on the camera. She had learned her lesson about backing up when they'd once lost all of their photographs from their holiday to France after Chris had formatted the card without asking her.

She scrolled through to the beginning of the card and flicked through some selfies of Chris pulling funny faces for the camera. Next came photographs of the two of them at a rugby match at Ellis Park, their faces brightly painted and waving vuvuzelas in the air. This was followed by photographs of a weekend away to Cape Town, a U2 concert, and a random mix of images from parties and outings with friends and family.

Michelle sped through the images until she reached some photos of the two of them at a friend's wedding. She and Chris were both dressed to the nines, smiles on their faces as they hugged each other tightly. She remembered that wedding. They had both had a little too much champagne and, after an evening of dancing, they had barely been able to keep their hands off each other when they got home. Later they had worked out that the baby had been conceived that night. Despite all her meticulous planning and all the medical assistance they'd paid for and received, the 'most fertile' dates ringed on the calendar, Michelle thought ruefully, in the end it had been in an atmosphere of genuine love that their baby had been created. She wished they could be those people again and just erase all the things that had happened since.

Michelle sighed and continued flicking through the remaining photographs.

Then she stopped. She let out a sudden cry, high, panic-stricken. The camera fell from her fingers, bounced once and lay on the carpet at her feet, the display facing upwards. Michelle stared down at it, incapable of movement, her face transfixed in pain.

It was a photograph of Maia.

chapter 22

THE SUDDEN FLASH of a bright light made Michelle look up, startled, from her laptop.

Maia was standing on the other side of the table. The little girl's eyes were wide open and a smile hovered about her lips as she tried to gauge whether or not she was in trouble. She was holding something behind her back.

'Did you take my picture?' Michelle asked.

Maia nodded slowly. She tried a broader smile, then thought better of it.

'Bring it here, Maia.' Michelle beckoned with her finger. 'Let me see what you have there.'

Maia came around the table and handed the digital camera to Michelle. She slid nervously onto the chair beside her. Michelle went through to the photo library and suppressed a smile when she saw that Maia had taken a photo of herself. The image showed her eyes filled with shock as she reacted to the flash.

'You know you shouldn't have taken the camera,' she began in her reprimanding voice, but when she saw the little girl's face fall, she relented. 'Never mind. We won't tell your mother. Come and sit on my lap and we'll take a photo together.'

Maia scrambled onto Michelle's lap and grinned up at her, happiness restored by Michelle's tone and the prospect of doing something fun. Michelle extended the camera and pointed it towards the two of them, putting her arm around Maia's shoulder and pulling her closer as she prepared to take the photograph.

'Now look into the camera – see, right there? – and say cheese.'

'Cheeeeeese!' Maia said and Michelle took the photo. This time when the flash went off Maia giggled hysterically and only stopped wriggling and laughing when Michelle turned the camera around and showed her the image. Maia had her eyes shut tightly, her chin turned up to the ceiling, her small white teeth in a fixed grimace. They both agreed they could do better.

'One more!' Maia said.

'But this time you need to look into the camera and smile.'

The next photograph came out much better than the first and the two of them laughed at the way they looked.

'Do you know what they call this?' Michelle asked the little girl.

Maia shook her head.

'A selfie.'

'Can we make another selfie?' Maia asked.

'We'll do one more and then I need to work,' Michelle said, holding the camera up while she waited for Maia to climb up closer to her. This time they pouted like fake models and the moment was captured in a flash of white light.

chapter 23

MAIA SMILED INNOCENTLY back at her as Michelle knelt down shakily to retrieve the camera from the study floor. The memories of that day came rushing into her mind like a tumultuous flood. Hands trembling, she flicked rapidly through the photographs she and Maia had taken together, each one a stab in her heart. Hidden below all the layers of stifling guilt she had carried for so many months was another emotion, one which she had not allowed herself to acknowledge until now.

She missed Maia. She missed her terribly.

Michelle had grown accustomed to the little girl's presence in the house over the years. She had been there when Rachel brought her home from the hospital in a taxi. She had bought toys and treats for her. Although Rachel tried to keep Maia from encroaching on their space in the house, it was inevitable that she would leave her mark and Michelle didn't mind. In fact she enjoyed finding the odd crayon or toy in the kitchen or behind one of the couches. Maia had occupied a special place in their lives. She especially missed the way the little girl's face lit up whenever Chris walked into a room.

As if it sensed that something was wrong, the baby turned inside her, causing Michelle to flinch in discomfort. She closed her eyes, breathed in deeply and exhaled slowly, trying to calm herself down through doing some of the breathing exercises she'd learned at the antenatal classes. When her heartbeat started to stabilise she opened her eyes again. She held the camera up so that she could look at the images once more, each one a finger pointing at her accusingly, confirming her guilt.

Michelle's thumb slid over the delete button and she watched as the icon of a trashcan appeared over the photograph of Maia, the options 'DELETE PHOTO' and 'CANCEL' below it. Her thumb hovered over the button that would confirm the action that would cause the image she was staring at to disappear for ever.

She pressed delete.

The photograph vanished instantly but was replaced by the next one.

Maia had her head cocked to the side and she was smiling shyly.

Delete.

Michelle moved through each of the photographs, picking up speed as she went.

Delete. Delete. Delete.

The action grew easier and soon she was rushing with the determination of a forest fire. The photographs of Maia quickly disappeared, as well as those Michelle had taken of them both. She didn't stop when she came to the blurry ones Maia had continued taking as she wandered through the house.

When she reached the final photograph Michelle paused. Her scorched earth policy was nearly complete. She didn't remember Maia taking this last one. It was a photo of her, sitting at the table with her cellphone against her ear. The expression on her face was one of pure excitement and delight, her free hand covering her mouth.

It was the phone call that had changed everything.

Michelle hit the delete button one last time and the photograph disappeared into darkness. She navigated through the camera menu, selected the format function and deleted every trace of that day from the memory card.

She couldn't take this any more. If Chris wasn't going to put an end to this toxic arrangement, then she was going to find a way to do it. She just needed a strategy. She needed to think.

Michelle placed the camera on the desk and left the study. She walked down the passage to their bedroom, where she sat at her dressing table, staring sightlessly at her reflection in the mirror, one finger tracing the intricate pattern on the lid of her jewellery box. The box had been a gift from Chris for their third wedding anniversary – hand crafted in leather. Chris was traditional like that. She took out the set of diamond earrings that had been another gift from her husband. The earrings were simple but expensive. She realised that she hadn't worn them in years. Holding them up to her ears, turning her head first to one side and then the other, she saw how they sparkled in the light from the window. Chris used to tell her she was beautiful. She didn't feel beautiful any more, inside or out.

It felt extra quiet in the house today for some reason. Rachel had said she wouldn't be back until late afternoon. Maybe she wasn't going to Home Affairs or whatever she'd said she was doing. Maybe she was going to an interview. Anyone could see that Rachel didn't want to be here any more than Michelle wanted her to be here. Perhaps Rachel was also about to take matters into her own hands.

A glance at the clock in the kitchen told Michelle it was still early. She took a key off a hanging rack beside the microwave, silencing the voice in her head by reminding herself of the end goal. This was for the greater good. If Michelle needed to be the person to rip the band-aid from the wound, then she would do it.

Outside there was a chill breeze and Michelle pulled her jersey closed. She inserted the master key into the lock on Rachel's living quarters, then hesitated. Even though she knew she was safe, she looked over her shoulder to make sure that she was alone. Once inside the room, she paused to let her eyes become accustomed to the gloom. She was keenly aware that she was an unwelcome presence in someone else's personal space, but she suppressed the feeling resolutely. She walked across to the small chest of drawers in the corner and pulled open a drawer. She felt through Rachel's clothes for where she might keep her valuables.

Nothing.

She stepped back and thought for a moment. Rachel did not have very much in the way of belongings and she was very tidy. Then her eye was caught by something underneath the bed. Michelle sat on the edge of the bed and felt about under it with her fingers until she coaxed the object out. It was a red tin, scuffed with age, with a brand of biscuits on the lid. She took it across to the table and opened it. The tin was filled with papers and cards. What sounded like loose coins rattled along the bottom. She lowered herself onto one of the wooden chairs and began curiously to sift through the tin's contents.

The first thing she saw was a photograph of Rachel with what must be her family in Mozambique. The faces were not familiar, of course, but Rachel had talked to her and Chris about her relatives there. Michelle put the photograph on the table and flipped through the rest of the papers and other items. The papers she put to one side, with the family photo. Michelle didn't really know what she was expecting to find but the tin didn't hold anything very interesting: old identity documents, some receipts, a blank Lotto card, a dirty old shell. As the tin emptied, so the pile beside her elbow on the table grew. Underneath all the paper stuff was a thin pile of R100 notes. As Michelle took them out a crumpled piece of paper slipped from the pile on the table and landed on the floor. She bent down to pick it up and when she saw what it was, any guilt around what her intrusion in this room meant vanished.

She sat leaning back in the chair for a few moments, getting her thoughts in order. Then, shaking her head and frowning, she put Rachel's things back in the tin just as she'd found them. She returned the tin to its place beneath the bed. Then she left the domestic quarters and walked back to the house, picked up her phone and dialled Chris's number. As she waited for him to answer, she went over the story that was now scripted in her head. She breathed in deeply, waiting, calm.

'Hey.'

'Chris,' Michelle said, her tone telling him that this was not a regular call merely to check in, 'I need to talk to you about something.'

She started talking in a measured voice. It was important that Chris understood exactly what she was saying and didn't interrupt her. She didn't want him to put this conversation down to raging hormones, as he'd been wont to do lately whenever she was upset about something.

When she'd finished, for a few minutes Chris didn't say anything. Michelle could sense him thinking down the phone line. Finally, he sighed and spoke.

'Michelle, how do you know that – '

'You know I'm not the kind of person who misplaces things,' Michelle said, cutting him off. She gave him another moment to process things. She had anticipated that Chris would be resistant to dealing with the situation and that she might need to apply some pressure to get him to move. Chris needed to be the one who dealt with this, not her. She lowered her voice, allowing empathy to come to the forefront. 'You also know we can't let something like this slide,' she said, her tone reasonable, even sorrowful. 'If we don't deal with it now, Chris, she'll just think she can do it again.'

'What do you want me to do? Fire her?'

'Chris, it's time.'

The line went quiet again and Michelle waited.

'Okay,' Chris said reluctantly. 'We'll talk to her when I get home. If you're right, we'll let her go.'

The afternoon sun had just started to dip when Rachel reached the Jordaans' street. The journey back from Home Affairs had taken longer than expected due to an argument between two rival taxi organisations and she had been forced to wait until order had been restored. With no child to rush back to, Rachel walked slowly, her body and soul tired from the challenges the week had brought.

This would be the last time that she would make the journey to Home Affairs with the security of an employment letter from the Jordaans, and her mind was reeling. How was she going to get cash to send home if she didn't have a job? As she walked along the street she saw Tapiwa sitting on the grass on the sidewalk, staring out at the traffic. Even though she wasn't in the mood to talk to anyone, Rachel made her way towards her and flopped down on the grass.

'Did you get it?' Tapiwa asked.

'Yes. I have another six months.'

'How was it?'

'Like it normally is.'

Tapiwa accepted Rachel's answer, knowing that they didn't need to go into detail about the experience they were both more than familiar with. Tapiwa reached into her bag and handed Rachel a packet of crisps, which Rachel accepted with a weary smile.

'Your body looks tired, my friend,' Tapiwa continued.

'I'm glad,' Rachel responded, placing a crisp in her mouth. 'It's no longer hiding what I feel like inside.'

The women sat in silence, idly watching the home-going cars driving past them, a silence that would have been filled by Maria had she not been away visiting family in Malawi that week.

'I haven't seen you at church in a while,' Tapiwa said.

Rachel nodded and smiled weakly, an expression which was response enough for her friend. The truth was Rachel hadn't been back to church since the funeral. The idea of travelling that far to listen to a man tell you to be more and do more was simply too much for her to handle.

'The pastor was talking on Sunday…'

Before Tapiwa could continue, Rachel heard footsteps behind her and turned to see Chris standing in the street, his work jacket in his hands.

'Rachel,' he said, interrupting their conversation. 'Could you come to the house when you're finished? Michelle and I need to talk to you about something.'

Rachel nodded and turned to say goodbye to Tapiwa while Chris strode home ahead of her. Rachel made her way down the driveway but before she had a chance to head to the main house she noticed that Chris and Michelle were waiting for her outside her room. Something was out of place. Rachel approached her room slowly, trying to work out what was going on.

Chris came straight to the point. Without meeting Rachel's eyes, he said: 'A pair of Michelle's earrings has gone missing.' He cleared his throat. 'Have you perhaps seen them anywhere?'

Rachel shook her head. She was puzzled. Michelle had many pairs of earrings. Which set was he referring to and why was he asking her? The only time she ever saw her employer's jewellery was when she dusted Michelle's dressing table and she hadn't done that in a few weeks now.

'I'm going to have to ask you if I can search your room,' Chris said, trying to be firm but clearly struggling.

Unsure what to make of this unusual tone for Chris, Rachel nodded shortly and took out her keys. She went inside, with Chris and Michelle right behind her. The room was as she had left it that morning, the air a little musty from it being closed up all day. She stood quietly by and watched as Chris looked around. He looked very uncomfortable, and when he asked her, awkwardly, to open the drawers that contained her clothing so that he could conduct his search, he looked abashed and still couldn't meet her eyes. When he went through to the bathroom to check the medicine cabinet, he left Rachel and Michelle alone in the room. The two women stood in silence, looking away from each other.

Chris came back empty handed and stood looking around him, much as Michelle had done a few hours earlier. Then he knelt down and looked under the bed. When he stood up he had Rachel's biscuit tin in his hand. He looked up at Rachel for permission and she nodded, watching expressionlessly as he pried the lid from the container and began to go through its contents.

Rachel knew that it was only a matter of time before he came across the ultrasound and she braced herself for Michelle's response. She looked down at her feet. She heard the sound of Chris pausing and his sharp intake of breath and she looked up. Chris was holding up her guilt. She also saw huge sadness in his eyes. Without saying a word he passed the ultrasound to Michelle, who took the photograph from him silently, her eyes still avoiding Rachel's. Michelle made no comment at all at the discovery; she didn't even look surprised.

Rachel looked back down at the floor as Chris continued going through the tin, but she felt less tense now. Her wrongdoing had been exposed. They couldn't know that some of the R100 notes at the bottom ...

'Rachel?'

Chris was holding out his hand. Cupped in his palm were two shiny objects that Rachel had only ever seen in Michelle's jewellery box. For just a second she was confused. Then, suddenly, she realised what was happening to her. This was Michelle's way of getting rid of her. She would have known Chris would never fire her so Michelle had needed to find a reason that left him with no other choice. Theft was inexcusable and, with her foreign status, there would be no trip to the courts or CCMA for her.

Rachel's instinct told her to defend herself, to tell Chris that she didn't know how the earrings had found their way into her biscuit tin among her private things. She wanted to confront Michelle right there and then, in front of him, and force her to confess to the crime. But the thought of it all left her exhausted, with a physical heaviness she could feel pushing down on her shoulders. She was just too tired to protest and, as this final weight was placed on her, she gave in to the feeling and chose the way of least resistance.

'I took them,' Rachel said.

The confession made no sense. She knew it and Michelle knew it too. But Rachel did not want to deny and nor did she want to beg. She could see that Michelle was thrown by the three simple words, as she would be.

Rachel looked Chris directly in the eye while she waited for him to respond. He seemed utterly bewildered.

'But why, Rachel?' Chris asked. 'You've never done anything like this before. What made you ...'

He was trying to provide her with a way out, an opportunity to say she had made a mistake or that she had lost her way and needed his help to get back on track. Chris would be able to handle someone in need of his mercy. But Rachel could not give him that. She looked back down at her feet and said nothing.

She heard Chris place the tin on the table and go and stand beside Michelle.

'You do realise that we can't continue to employ you?' His voice was harder now.

Rachel nodded, still staring down at her feet.

'I'll have to ask you to leave the property – I'll give you till Friday.'

Rachel nodded acceptance. She waited for her employers to leave the room. She looked up as they exited, her eyes briefly crossing Michelle's as she walked out behind Chris.

Michelle had won but in that second when their eyes met Rachel saw that her victory had come at a price. In that split second of eye contact she could see that Michelle derived no pleasure from what she had just orchestrated. This certain knowledge did nothing to soften Rachel's heart towards her employer but it helped her understand. Michelle had done it so that she could move forward. Just like Rachel, Michelle was trapped, too, and so she had done what she needed to do to free herself, even if by doing so she knew she was destroying the only chance Rachel had left to stay in South Africa and support her family.

Michelle followed Chris into the house, clutching the ultrasound and earrings in her hands as she tried to catch up with him. She was surprised at how swiftly he had dealt with the situation. She had expected him to take his time, to try and figure out the best way to handle it. She closed the door behind them and followed Chris's trail of discarded work clothes that led to the kitchen, automatically picking up his jacket and tie and anticipating the conversation that would follow.

Chris was standing in the breakfast nook, a beer in his hand, looking out into the garden. He turned to face Michelle and she saw how his eyes were filled with sadness. He was about to say something when his phone started ringing.

'It's the office,' he said, glancing at the screen. 'Hannes.' He put the phone to his ear. 'What is it?'

Michelle half-listened as Chris talked to his colleague but she could see from his deflated bearing that whatever it was, it wasn't good news. She smoothed out the crumpled ultrasound and stuck it back in its place on the fridge door. She set the diamond earrings down on the counter top and proceeded to move around the kitchen straightening things until she heard Chris finish with the call.

'They want me to go to Durban for two days,' Chris said, exasperated. 'There's a problem with one of the buildings and the client wants face time with me. I can see if Lukas can go but he has no clue ...'

'It's okay. Go.'

Chris paused and looked at her, his eyes trying to read if she was being honest.

It wasn't the best of news but, after the way he had handled the situation with Rachel, Michelle reckoned it would be better if she didn't make any waves for him right now.

'Seriously,' Michelle added. 'It's fine.'

'Durban's only an hour away. If there's any trouble, I'll be on the plane right back.'

Michelle nodded and Chris picked up the phone to call Hannes back.

'Do you need me to help you with anything before you go?' Michelle asked as he waited for the call to connect.

'No. I'll just throw a few things into a bag later.'

Chris turned round and looked out of the window into the garden again. Michelle stood beside him. The swimming pool was now so green you couldn't see the bottom.

'We'll have to drain it,' Chris said. 'The water's too dirty for us to save now.'

Rachel sat at her wooden table with a red pen in her hand, an open newspaper in front of her. The madness of the day was drawing to an end with the same object that had ushered it in: the Jobs section of the classifieds. The only difference was that she was the one making the red marks now, looking for employment in the employment offered section, which was considerably shorter than the section of people looking for work.

She scanned through the offers, realising with each one she read that the set-up she had with the Jordaans was a rare one. Most of the salaries on offer were half of what she was currently earning and many did not include on site accommodation. Most people in her situation would end up staying in shacks in the informal settlements that had sprung up on the outskirts of the city and take taxis in to the suburbs. Rachel shook her head as the reality of what was available took hold.

She had managed to raise the money that was needed for her father's medication by using up just about all her savings and selling the ring and her cellphone, but now she had nothing but the small pile of R100 notes to buffer herself. She anticipated that she would get one last paycheck out of the Jordaans but if she didn't find work within the next two weeks, she would be in trouble.

Rachel put the pen down and looked across at the urn that contained Maia's ashes, wondering how much she could get for the container, then shaking her head at the fact that she was even asking herself that question.

She was trapped.

His bag packed and presentation ready, Chris tossed some of the pillows from his bed in the guest room onto the floor, pulled the duvet back and climbed in. His head was pounding from the stress of the day. He closed his eyes in an attempt to alleviate the pain in his temple. He couldn't believe that things with Rachel had come to this. Stealing was something so far removed from her character – or what he'd thought he knew of her character – that he was struggling to accept that she had taken the earrings, despite her admission. He heard footsteps in the passage. Michelle was standing in the doorway, a mug of tea in her hands, ready to make her way to bed.

'You comfortable?'

Chris plumped up his pillow and nodded. 'Are you going to bed?'

'Yes,' Michelle replied. 'Do you need anything from the bedroom?'

Chris shook his head.

'Why don't you come and sleep there?' Michelle suggested. 'You know this bed always hurts your back.'

'I'm leaving so early in the morning it's easier if I sleep here.'

'Okay,' Michelle said. 'Make sure you give me a call when you land.'

'I will.'

With nothing left to say, Michelle stepped back into the passage.

'Good night, Chris,' she said.

'Night, Michelle. Sleep well.'

Michelle turned off the passage light and Chris lay back down. He felt for the switch on the bedside lamp and, picking up his smartphone, he saw that he had a message from Anja on WhatsApp.

I'll see you with coffee at arrivals at 8:15 Boss!

Two sugars :) Chris typed back.

He set the alarm on his phone for 04:30, a wake-up time that was much too early for his liking.

The following morning brought with it an uneasy calm. Michelle had decided to wake up early so that she could make breakfast for Chris before he left for the airport. It was still dark outside but the arrival of spring made the task more bearable. Soon the smell of coffee and bacon filled the house. Chris had looked surprised at such industry but he gave Michelle a smile and took a piece of bacon from the pan and a piece of buttered toast.

'Thanks, but I'm already late,' he said. 'Call me if you need anything.'

His coffee stood untouched.

'We'll be fine,' Michelle said, her hands on her belly. 'You'd better get moving if you're going to beat the traffic.'

'Are you sure you'll be okay?'

'Go,' Michelle said. She handed Chris his jacket. 'I'll be fine as long as you're back on Friday so that I don't have to deal with Rachel alone.'

Chris kissed her on the lips and took his jacket from her.

'I'll call you when I land.'

Michelle walked her husband to the door and waved goodbye as he got into his car and reversed up the driveway. While this was no different to their usual morning routine these past months, she felt incredibly isolated as she went back to the kitchen.

With Rachel obviously not coming in to clean the house today, it was up to Michelle to clear things up, which had never been her favourite activity. As she leaned across the table to collect Chris's plate and still-full mug, she heard a crash. Her swollen belly had knocked the sugar bowl off the table. Hugo gave a shocked yelp and scuttled to his basket. Michelle stepped cautiously around the brown granules and shards of glass, trying to avoid getting cut while she looked for something to use to clean up the mess.

Where did Rachel keep the vacuum cleaner? Taking a chance, she made her way to the broom cupboard and there it was. She pulled it out and dragged it across the kitchen floor. Halfway through pulling out the electrical cable, she saw that it was a two-pronged plug. A quick scan of the outlets in the kitchen told her that she'd have to go searching for an adaptor. She couldn't think where there might be a spare but knew there was one in the study because her speakers and phone charger were connected to it. Sighing, she walked down the passage and crawled uncomfortably under her desk. She yanked the adaptor out and reversed out on her knees. Breathing hard and using the corner of the desk for leverage, she got clumsily to her feet and returned to the kitchen where, for the first time in years, she used the vacuum cleaner (which her parents had given to her and Chris when they moved into the house) to suck up the sugar and glass. She couldn't be bothered to put it back in the cupboard, but she took the adaptor back to the study. By the time she had shoved it into the wall socket under the desk, she was exhausted and her lower back was aching.

Rachel had spent her last few days at the Jordaans packing her bags and trying to see what she could get rid of before she left. Tapiwa had offered to keep some of her things for her until she found a new home but, as she looked at her two suitcases, she realised that she actually didn't own that much and wouldn't need to take up the offer. The bed and most of the furniture belonged to the Jordaans and she had given all of Maia's toys and clothes away the month after her passing to the children's home that the church ran from its property.

She had managed to arrange two interviews for the following week but now, with nearly all her stuff packed, she found she had nothing left to do but wait for her last day at the Jordaans to arrive. She had R500 to her name, barely enough to pay for accommodation anywhere, and had resigned herself to the fact that she would probably have to stay in the park, the one where she used to take Maia to play and where she had seen the little girl who was not Maia playing on the slide. Tapiwa's room was half the size of hers and Maria was still away, so the park it would have to be, at least until she managed to secure accommodation. She would clean herself in the public washrooms with the soap she had and she would try her best to keep her clothes from getting dirty so that she would be presentable for her interviews. Fortunately, the warmth of spring meant that the nights would not be as cold as they had been a few weeks ago but the idea of sleeping alone in a park was not something Rachel wanted to dwell on all the same.

At least Maia wasn't here to experience any of this.

It was late afternoon when she heard the doorbell ring and a few seconds later the side gate at the top of the driveway opened. She went over to the window and pulled back the curtain. A young black woman, roughly the same age as Rachel, had entered the property and was walking down the driveway. She stopped halfway down and look around, obviously trying to work out exactly where to go.

Her replacement.

Michelle was certainly not wasting any time.

Before Rachel was able to duck back, the woman saw her standing at the window and waved hello at her, but instead of returning the greeting she quickly drew the curtain. She sat down abruptly on her bed. She could hear Michelle's voice now, calling out pleasantly and directing the woman towards the house. Rachel waited for silence to return to the driveway before taking up her viewing point at the window once more.

In the distance she heard the low rumble of thunder, an ominous sound, but one that heralded the first rain of the season. She opened the window and breathed in deeply, the peppery scent of the approaching storm sharp in her nostrils.

Johannesburg was famous for its electrical storms, huge celestial displays of light and noise that would rip through the skies and could wreak considerable havoc. She had even seen trees uprooted and nearly every summer there would be reports of flooding somewhere, usually affecting the overcrowded informal settlements close to the rivers. Having never experienced these kinds of storms in Inhassoro, with lightning searing across the sky and the sharp crack of thunder that followed it, Rachel had a wary respect for their power but more than that, storms terrified her. Despite Michelle and Chris's reassurances over the years, she'd never come to terms with them. She steadfastly refused to go outside when a storm was raging, to the point that she would sit most of a storm out on a chair in her room, or in the kitchen if she was still working, or in her bed so that her feet were not touching the ground.

As she watched the dust swirl in a sudden gust of wind, a sure sign that a storm was coming, she was gripped by a sense of dread. The sun hadn't quite gone down yet but the sky had grown dark and threatening. Whether she liked it or not, a big storm was about to hit. Michelle opened the gate for Lucy to leave the property and waited for it to close before she returned to the study. The woman had seemed nice enough. She came from Blantyre in Malawi, had no children, and had been in South Africa for over ten years. She came with impeccable references from two families, the most recent of which had emigrated to Australia. She seemed capable of doing all the tasks that would be required of her and was satisfied with the wages Michelle had put on the table.

Most importantly, she was able to start on Monday. She told Michelle she could arrange to move in over the weekend, once Rachel had left.

Michelle decided to call Chris. There was no message on her phone to say he was safely in Durban and it was getting late. Whenever either of them travelled on business, they had an agreement that they would text each other when they landed, but perhaps his flight had been delayed. She let the phone ring for a while and was about to hang up when Chris answered. He sounded out of breath.

'Hey!'

'You get there okay?' Michelle asked.

'*Ja*,' Chris replied, his voice surrounded by traffic. 'Sorry. It took a while at the car hire place and I've only just checked in at the hotel. I went straight to my first meeting from the airport. And now I have to get ready to have drinks and dinner with the client in fifteen minutes.'

'I just had a lady come through to interview for the position,'

Rachel told him.

'What position?' Chris asked.

'The maid's,' Michelle replied patiently.

'Oh yes. And?'

'She seems okay. Doesn't speak great English but she came with good references. She can start on Monday.'

'That sounds good. What's her situation?'

'Malawian. No kids or heavy family connections.'

Thunder rolled in the distance and Michelle walked to the window to try and gauge how far away the storm was. The sun was still shining but black clouds were brewing just below the treeline, the wind carrying them quickly towards Parkhurst, it looked like.

'There's a storm's brewing,' Michelle said, closing the window.

'Remember to unplug the electronics if there's lightning,' Chris said. 'The last thing we need is to lose another modem.'

'I will, don't worry.'

'Listen – I've got to go now but I'll call you after dinner if it doesn't go on too late.'

'All right,' Michelle said. 'Listen, I've been thinking. When you get back maybe we should decide on a colour for the baby's room.'

'Sounds like a plan.' Chris sounded distracted. 'Let's talk about it when I get back.'

'Sure,' Michelle said.

Somewhere in the house an open window was banging against its frame. This one was going to be a big storm. Before she went to investigate and sort out the unsettling noise, she noticed that there was only one bar of battery left on her phone so she plugged it into the charger on the desk. In the kitchen she saw Hugo shivering in his basket. He didn't like storms. When there were bad ones he would squeeze beneath the sofa in the lounge. He looked up at Michelle with fear-filled eyes and whimpered. She went over and scratched him behind his ears, murmuring some soothing words.

Chris pushed his phone into his pocket and looked around. Anja was standing a few feet away. He smiled and strode towards her, scanning the busy restaurant for the clients they were supposed to be meeting up with. He spotted them sitting in the corner at a four-seater table, two Afrikaans men in their mid-thirties who, judging from the empty beer bottles on the table, looked as though they had been sitting there for a while.

'There they are,' Chris said. He placed a hand on Anja's lower back to get her attention and guide her towards them.

'Showtime,' Anja said. Smiling, she walked ahead of Chris to the table, hand outstretched. 'Good evening, gentlemen,' she said as the two men hastily rose to their feet. 'I'm Anja.'

Rachel turned on the light, even though it was still relatively early. The storm clouds had blocked out the setting sun completely now and she could hear the wind scratching at the door, rattling it against the frame which was doing its best to keep it in place. She made herself a cup of tea before unplugging the kettle along with the rest of the electrical items in the room, as Chris had instructed her to do many years ago. She began to fold the last of her clothes and pack them into the suitcase that was still open on the floor for all the last minute things she'd put in tomorrow. The room was practically bare. Soon there would be no trace of her left at all, her presence like footprints on the beach swallowed up by the incoming tide. It would be as though she had never existed.

Chris burst out laughing as Anja finished the joke she was telling the table; Werner and Johan joined in at the punch line. What he had expected to be a continuation of the somewhat tense business meeting earlier in the day had in fact turned into a drinking evening with very little discussion around the problem with the building plans.

The waiter came to clear away the empty glasses and Werner looked enquiringly around the table. Anja and Johan nodded to another round and, even though his head was spinning, Chris did the same. He sat back in his chair, trying to assess how drunk he was. Pretty drunk, he concluded.

He felt his leg against Anja's but did nothing to move it away, waiting to see if she would. She didn't and, as Johan started to tell them another story and the next round of drinks arrived, his reservations began to melt away.

Michelle opened the cupboard in the baby's room and placed a pile of neatly folded babygros on the top shelf. They were gifts from the baby shower and, as she looked around the rest of the room, she realised that they were almost ready for the baby to come. The crib was in place, the changing station was ready and the framed pictures were in two neat piles, ready to be hung on the walls as soon as they'd been painted. The only thing that was left for them to do was assemble the mobile that Karlien had given them and hang it above the crib. She decided that now was as good a time as any.

Sitting down on the floor, she opened the box and began to lay the pieces out in front of her. Hugo, who had bravely left his basket and followed her down the passage, was sniffing around as he tried to see what she was busy with. He settled down on the carpet beside her with a deep sigh. Outside the wind blew strongly in regular waves and gusts. Michelle heard the dull thump of a trashcan being blown over.

The elevator doors opened on the fifth floor and Chris and Anja stumbled out, laughing. Anja had her shoes in her hand. She was walking slowly and couldn't stop giggling. They peered up and down the quiet passage to see if anyone else was around. Chris could barely walk straight. His face was numb. He stumbled forward as Anja grabbed hold of his shoulder in an attempt to steady herself. The action set both of them wobbling and then crashing to the floor where they lay on the plush carpet, giggling and shushing each other.

'I don't know how we're going to explain all those bottles to the guys in accounts,' Chris said as he used the wall to help him get to his feet. He picked up his laptop bag and then held his hand out to Anja. She hiccupped and giggled and allowed him to pull her up.

'We? You're the one who ordered them,' she said.

'And you're the one who kept drinking them. Where the hell do you fit all that booze in that tiny body of yours?'

'Right here,' Anja said, smacking her rear playfully.

Chris squinted at the numbers on the doors and, once he had orientated himself, led the way. He stopped when he got to his room. Anja's was directly opposite.

'Here we are,' he said, patting his pockets in an attempt to locate his access card. All he could find was his phone and his wallet. He started rummaging through his laptop bag while Anja opened the door to her room.

'What are you doing?' Anja asked. She tossed her shoes into the room and turned around.

'Looking for my damn card.'

Chris put the bag down on the carpet and started fumbling through his pockets again, the alcohol slowing down his search somewhat. Anja watched him, laughing quietly. Then she stepped over and opened his jacket to check his inside pocket, poking him first in his ribs.

'No, man, that tickles!' Chris said, doubling over and pulling back, which only made Anja laugh louder and poke him again.

'Shhhh! You're going to wake everyone,' she said, putting a finger to her lips.

Chris bit his lip and let Anja's fingers go from his inside jacket to his shirt pocket, but his eyes warned her not to tickle him again. Anja had stopped laughing. She moved her hands to his pants pockets. Chris breathed in deeply as she put her hand inside the right one, dug around and came out with the keys to the rental car. She held them up for him to see and jiggled them in the air.

'I wonder what we'll find in the other one?' she asked with an innocent smile.

Chris's heart was thudding in his chest but he didn't move as

Anja slowly reached for the other pocket. All playfulness between them had disappeared. He recognised the line they were crossing. His body responded to the energy between them and as Anja held her body against his, he felt his self-control starting to slip away.

He leaned in and was about to kiss her when they heard a loud 'ping' and the doors to the elevator opening. Chris and Anja jumped away from each other as a middle-aged businessman with a large suitcase exited, looked at the numbers on the doors of the rooms closest to the elevator and, once orientated, came walking towards them, dragging the heavy piece of luggage behind him. Chris exhaled deeply and Anja stepped back into the doorway to her room while they waited for the man to pass.

The man had a round, sweaty face. He greeted them and stopped at a door two rooms down from Anja's. As he fiddled in his pocket and drew out his access card, Chris and Anja held each other's eyes.

The few moments' interruption allowed Chris mentally to assess what was about to happen and to take stock. It wasn't a difficult picture to assemble. His wife was alone in another city about to have their first child and he was about to cheat on her. As the sweaty man did battle with his card and the door of his hotel room the stakes and what Chris stood to lose became clearer to him. The thought sobered him up quickly. He dropped his eyes from Anja's and leaned against the door. As he did so he felt something in the back pocket of his pants and knew immediately that it was his access card.

The man had finally got his door open. He pushed his bag into his room and they heard the click of the lock. The corridor returned to silence. Chris looked across the divide between him and Anja, who cocked her head to the side as she waited for him to make the expected next move.

Chris smiled weakly and held up the card for her to see, embarrassed that he had led her on and was now backing out. 'Found it.'

Anja nodded and smiled, acknowledging that things were not going to go any further than this tonight.

'Goodnight, Chris,' she said and stepped backwards into her room.

'Night,' Chris responded. He watched as she closed the door on him.

Chris turned around and slid his access card into the slot in his door and heard the lock click. The door popped open. He walked inside and closed the door behind him, turning the manual lock as well, more for himself than for Anja. The room was simple and clean. The digital clock beside the bed told him that it was just after 21:30, not actually as late as he'd thought. Opening the sliding door to the balcony, he saw that he had an unobscured view of the beachfront. The waves of the warm Indian Ocean crashed softly just a few hundred metres away.

He took out his phone and scrolled through his address book until he reached Michelle's name. He hit dial and while he waited for it to connect, appreciated the sound of the waves as they crashed against each other and thumped onto the shore. The call went straight to voicemail. Michelle had probably gone to bed already. He listened to her message as it played out and waited for the tone to beep before he spoke.

'Hey, it's me,' he said as the fresh wind from the ocean hit his face. 'Just wanted to say I'm thinking of you … both of you. I've got some meetings in the morning but I'll be home in the evening if everything goes according to plan. Love you.'

Michelle was still sitting on the floor of the baby's room trying to assemble Karlien's pastel mobile. It was proving to be far more complicated than she'd thought. It was very dark outside now. The night sky was filled with flashes of lightning every few minutes, predictably followed by growls of thunder. She could also hear rain pattering against the window. Hugo whined and edged closer to her. Michelle stroked his head. She was about to return her attention to the frustrating mobile when lightning struck again, impossibly close this time and making her heart leap into her throat. At the same instant the house was plunged into pitch darkness. Hugo let out a yelp and burrowed his head in Michelle's lap.

'Shit,' Michelle said. It must have hit the mains. She pushed Hugo off her and got awkwardly to her feet.

She wasn't afraid but Chris usually handled this kind of situation and she wished he was here. She stood for a moment trying to think where the electrical box was. She knew they had a torch but she had no idea where that was either. Feeling lightheaded from standing up too quickly, she waited for the dizziness to pass before navigating through the dark house towards the kitchen. Hugo was right behind her.

Outside the storm was growing and coming even closer, if that was possible. Flares of lightning and the crack of thunder that followed were almost simultaneous now. As Michelle went into the kitchen she saw that the blinds were still up and she had also forgotten to close one of the windows beside the back door. The rain was coming in. She could hear it tinkling into the empty fruit bowl on the table in the breakfast nook. Treading carefully so as not to slip on the wet floor, she went across and closed the window. Another flash of lightning momentarily blinded her and she stopped while her eyes adjusted before she turned around. Then she made her way to the broom cupboard where Rachel kept her mops and brooms. She'd remembered this was also where the electrical box was. Flicking the switches up and down, she waited for light to return to the house but nothing happened. 'Shit,' Michelle said again.

She knew there were candles in the drawer by the sink and she turned around to make her way back towards it. A vicious bolt of lightning slashed violently through the sky, eerily lighting up the back garden, and Michelle's heart began to beat faster. For a moment she felt dizzy and disorientated and she put out a hand to steady herself on the cupboard door. Hugo was whining and frantically running around her legs in circles while the thunder crashed and boomed and the house felt as if it was being shaken to its foundations.

As she took a sideways step to avoid the terrified dog, Michelle tripped on something solid and stumbled forward, only to feel her ankle caught in something else. The bloody vacuum cleaner! She screamed as she went down and just before she slammed into the tiled kitchen floor, instinctively she tried to twist her body to the side but landed belly first instead on the hard floor. She felt a sharp stab of pain rip through her stomach and gasped.

Michelle immediately rolled over onto her side in an attempt to take her weight off the baby and then lay where she was, exhaling slowly as she tried to assess the state of her body. Hugo was by her side, licking at her face. Michelle pushed him away and, groaning painfully, began to push herself up. She seemed to be intact.

She leaned forward and climbed onto her hands and knees, letting out a sharp cry as a sudden wave of pain moved through her body. She must have hurt herself. She hoped she hadn't hurt the baby too.

Using the counter for support, Michelle pulled herself up and just then she felt a pop between her legs. When she looked down she could see that her pants were stained dark and soaking wet. She gingerly touched the area, the texture of the liquid revealing that this was not from the rain that had come in from the open window.

Her water had broken.

Rachel had climbed into bed as soon as the power had gone out, wrapping the blue blanket around her head as she listened to the heavens open and the rain descend on the property. She flinched with every lightning bolt and buried herself deeper into the safety of her bed, trying every trick she could think of to distance herself from the chaos raging outside.

She forced her mind to focus on her vague plans for the next day – Friday: the day she would be leaving the Jordaans' home for good, taking all that she owned with her. She had been instructed to be gone before midday. In a few hours it would be morning and, God willing, the rain would have stopped by then. At least she had a roof over her head tonight.

Thunder boomed again, reverberating through the room, and the wind shrieked, a long high-pitched wail. Rachel thought it sounded just like someone screaming.

Michelle shifted her stomach heavily and made her way to the landline. She had better call Dr Pieterse. Maybe even an ambulance. But first she needed reassurance from her gynaecologist. Luckily she had written her number down on a piece of paper and stuck it next to the phone. She picked up the receiver and put it to her ear.

The phone was dead.

She took a deep breath and exhaled slowly. Then another wave of pain hit and she dropped back down to her hands and knees in an attempt to alleviate it. Somehow she would have to get to the study, where her iPhone was charging. She started to crawl towards the passage, gasping for air and having to stop every couple of minutes. It was very dark and her progress was slow. Eventually, however, she made it into the study. Outside the rain beat down on the roof and lashed at the windows. Managing to pull herself up onto her knees, her fingers scrabbled on the desk for her phone. Using one hand, the other holding her belly, she disconnected the phone from the charger and sank onto the carpet. She pushed the home button to activate the phone but the screen didn't light up. She hit the instrument against her palm and tried again. Still the screen remained dead. She got down onto her knees again and followed the length of the cable and, in the dingy recess of the desk, saw that while it was plugged into the wall she hadn't turned the plug switch back on after she'd used the adaptor for the vacuum cleaner.

'No, no, no, no, no,' Michelle pleaded. 'Not now.'

She tried pushing the button one last time in the hope that by some fluke the phone would start up again but her hope was rewarded only by another searing pain that caused her to double over and cry out for relief from what she could only assume now were contractions.

The baby was coming whether she was ready or not.

chapter 24

MICHELLE LOOKED UP from her laptop. Bored with the camera game, Maia was standing staring at her. She was also clicking her tongue against her teeth, a sound that was making it impossible for Michelle to focus on the email she was trying to compose. Her phone started ringing and she reached across for it, smiling as she saw on the screen who it was.

It was Dr Pieterse's office.

Hugo started barking at the persistent ringtone. Michelle looked over to Maia, who had stopped her tongue-clicking noise and had replaced it with flicking her Mermaid Barbie's long hair at Hugo's nose, which made his barking shriller.

'Maia,' Michelle said, 'why don't you take Hugo outside so that I can answer this call?'

Maia perked up at the idea and, nodding enthusiastically, called for Hugo to follow her to the front door. Michelle called out after her: 'Make sure you stay in the front garden by the tree' – she pointed in the direction of the main entrance.

'Hello, Michelle speaking.'

'Michelle, hi. It's Dr Pieterse here. How're you doing?'

'I don't know,' Michelle responded, waving at Maia as she skipped out of the room, Hugo skidding behind her on the polished floor. 'I guess I'm waiting for you to tell me.'

Dr Pieterse chuckled. 'Well, I have your test results in front of me,' she said.

'And? The suspense has been driving me crazy!'

Michelle stood up and began pacing around. In the kitchen she noticed that the door to the back garden was open. She walked towards it and pulled it closed while she waited for Dr Pieterse to give her the news. After a weekend of waiting, she was ready for some certainty. She walked slowly back to the big wooden table.

'I'm happy to say that, according to your blood tests, you're between five to six weeks' pregnant,' Dr Pieterse said.

A rush of joy filled Michelle's heart. Her hands trembling with excitement, she almost dropped the phone. The years of trying, the hopes and the prayers – now it was finally happening.

'What?' Michelle exclaimed. 'Are you sure? Are you absolutely sure?'

Dr Pieterse laughed. 'Well, that's what the tests say.'

'You have no idea what this means to us.'

'I think I do, Michelle, and I'm glad I could be the bearer of good news this time. Now, before you go, we need to set up an appointment within the next week so that we can do a proper examination and see how the baby is doing. I'll let you do that with Gill in a moment, when we're done here, shall I?'

'Thank you so much.'

'Only a pleasure. I'll patch you through to Gill shortly. In the meantime I want you to start taking a pregnancy vitamin and mineral supplement. You'll find a range of these at your local pharmacy. Whatever brand you choose, just make sure it has folic acid and calcium in it.'

Hugo was barking loudly outside, the annoying yapping making it difficult for Michelle to hear. She walked down the passage to the other side of the house.

'Sorry, Doctor,' she said. 'I didn't hear that last bit? Our dog was barking. You said it must have folic acid and ...?'

'Calcium.'

'Got it. Anything else I should do?'

'Nothing right now. I'll put you through to Gill and she'll set up your appointment.'

Michelle thanked the doctor again, a broad smile spreading across her face as she waited to be connected to the front desk. Hugo was still barking manically in the garden. Something was upsetting him. Michelle started back towards the kitchen to see what the fuss was about.

'Hugo!' she shouted on the way, the phone pressed against her thigh. 'Shut up!'

She was almost at the window when Dr Pieterse's secretary came on the line and she shifted her attention back to the call, changing direction at the same time. It would be a little quieter in the lounge.

'Hi, Gill, it's Michelle Jordaan here.'

'Congratulations, Michelle, I heard the good news just now,' Gill said. There was a genuine and heartfelt tone in her voice.

‘Thank you, Gill. Dr Pieterse said I needed to book an appointment with her. Can you tell me what’s available next week?’

‘Sure.’ Michelle could hear pages being turned. ‘How is Thursday at 10:30?’

‘That’s perfect,’ Michelle said, without needing to check the calendar on her laptop, which was still on the table. Whatever she was doing next Thursday could be cancelled. ‘Do I need to bring anything?’

‘Just yourself.’

They said goodbye and Michelle hung up the phone. She saw that her hands were still trembling. Excitement bubbled up in her chest as she scrolled down to Chris’s name on her call list.

Outside Hugo was not letting up, the over-excited yapping close to fever pitch. This barking wasn’t funny. If the habit wasn’t curbed, it wouldn’t be long before the neighbours began to complain. Michelle made a mental note to order the shock collar that she’d seen online and if Chris didn’t like it, he was going to have to take the dog for training.

‘Hugo!’ Michelle shouted again as she hit dial. ‘For goodness sake!’

There was a mirror on one of the walls in the lounge. She gazed at her reflection trying to see if she looked any different. She certainly looked joyful and she smiled at herself unashamedly.

‘Hello, babe.’

The sound of Chris’s voice caused her suddenly to choke up with emotion and she almost couldn’t speak.

‘*Lief* …’ she began.

‘What’s wrong? Has something happened?’

‘The tests came back today,’ Michelle said and she started to laugh. 'We're having a baby.'

'What?'

'Dr Pieterse just called … She said – ' Before she had a chance to finish her sentence she heard Chris let out a whoop that was followed by a laugh filled with life and pleasure.

'We're having a baby!' Chris called out to the people around him before returning his attention to Michelle. 'We're having a *baby*?'

'Yes.'

'We're going to be a … wait a second. Are you okay? Do you need anything?'

'No, I'm fine. Really.' Michelle replied, laughing at his concern. 'Maybe just some rat poison to shut your damn dog up.'

Chris chuckled. 'I'm coming home right now,' he said. 'What do you want to eat? Something strange, right?'

Michelle just kept laughing. She thought this was probably the happiest day of her life.

'I'll see you now,' Chris said.

'Don't say anything until we've told my – '

Michelle was cut off by the dial tone and she shook her head, smiling.

' – parents,' she finished. As she said the word, the news began to sink in. 'We're going to be parents,' she whispered to her reflection in the mirror.

Hugo had finally stopped barking and Michelle used the moment of peace to allow everything to take shape in her mind. It was happening for them at last. She scrolled through her contact list again and went straight to her mother's number. She hit the green call button and waited.

'Mom …'

chapter 25

MICHELLE CRAWLED TOWARDS the front door. When she got there, she reached up onto the cabinet beside it to grab her car keys. With great effort, she pulled herself up and got the door open. Hugo hovered closely, whimpering, trying to work out why his mistress was in such distress.

A blast of wind and rain hit Michelle in the face. Fumbling with the house keys and doing her best to keep Hugo inside with her foot, she unlocked the steel security gate and stepped out into the rain. She hobbled up the driveway towards her car.

Then another contraction hit, stopping her in her tracks and causing her to gasp in pain. She waited for it to subside and then, gritting her teeth, she resumed her journey to the car, deactivating the alarm with the key as she approached it. She was already soaked to the skin. Heavy drops of rain stung her cheeks and she could hardly see where she was going. Taking deep breaths, she opened the car door, settled herself into the driver's seat and tried to put the key into the ignition. Her hands were shaking from cold and pain and her fingers felt numb and clumsy. She missed the slot and the keys fell from her hands. She heard them clatter onto the driveway and cursed herself for not closing the car door first.

The rain was really pelting down and the sloping driveway was awash as water flowed down it in steady rivulets from the road outside. Michelle got out of the car and crouched down to feel beneath the car for the keys. Mercifully, she saw them just within reach and took hold of them firmly, concentrating on slow, deep breathing and willing the next contraction to stay away until she was safely on the road to the hospital. This time she managed to start the vehicle without any problem and she put the car into reverse, activating the access remote, and watching in the rear view mirror for the electronic gate at the top of the driveway to slide open.

It didn't.

Michelle pressed the button again and began to reverse slowly. She looked over her shoulder.

The security gate hadn't moved an inch.

Moaning in frustration and fear, Michelle slammed her hands against the steering wheel, causing the horn to go off with loud insisting hooting. She put the car in neutral and pulled up the handbrake. The motor for the gate must have been taken out by the lightning too. She turned off the engine and sat thinking. Probably she should have been timing her contractions; or maybe it was just as well she hadn't been. She was scared enough now as it was.

Wearily, she climbed back out of the car, not even noticing the rain this time. She plodded up towards the electronic gate, her shoes splashing through the river that used to be their driveway. Chris had shown her how to bypass the motor when they had first moved in but she hadn't paid much attention to his instructions. And now, as she peered through the darkness at the mechanism, she realised that she had no clue how to get the gate open manually. There was a large lock on the motor cover anyway to prevent thieves from accessing it. In vain she tried to fit one of the keys on her keyring to the lock. None of them worked, nor even fitted into the lock.

Bracing herself, she tugged on the gate with all her might, hoping that brute force would cause the barrier to move along the sliding rails. The gate did not budge. Perhaps it was the physical exertion that triggered it, but another sudden contraction took her breath away and she screamed in pain and frustration. Grabbing onto her stomach, Michelle tried to make her way back to the car but the pain was too much. Once more she dropped onto her hands and knees and just stayed there, head hanging, her sodden hair and the relentless pouring rain completely obscuring her vision. She let out a primitive moan. She couldn't move. Her body was paralysed by the pain. And she had no way of getting help.

chapter 26

MICHELLE FINISHED THE call to her mother. She couldn't stop smiling. Looking down at her flat stomach, she found it difficult to believe that there was another life growing inside of her. She tried to sense its presence.

The clock in the kitchen told her it was almost lunchtime. Maia must be getting hungry. She opened the cupboard to see what she might make for her. A sandwich? Soup?

'Maia!' she called out. 'What do you want for lunch?'

Her question echoed through the house and while she waited for a reply, she took out a loaf of bread. When she heard no response she called out more loudly. She realised that the child probably couldn't hear her from the front garden.

Michelle listened again and when she still heard nothing she walked through the house, putting her head into each one of the rooms. Empty. No Maia. Mildly annoyed now, she opened the front door and walked up the driveway. Where could the child have got to? Hiding maybe? Hide and seek was still one of Maia's favourite games.

'Maia! It's lunchtime!' she shouted. 'Come on, now!'

She went around the front garden to Rachel's room to see if the little girl was there. Another unanswered call prompted Michelle to stop and listen.

Silence. What was wrong with the silence?

Hugo. The dog had stopped barking but where was he? Could Maia have taken him for a walk out in the road? She looked towards the side gate at the top of the driveway but it was closed. Maia wouldn't have known how to open it anyway.

'Maia …?' Michelle called, her heartbeat accelerating as she walked along the side of the house and into the back garden. 'Where are you hiding? Hugo?'

The trees that lined the side of the house were overgrown and as Michelle made her way down the stone pathway the wind picked up and blew in gusts around her, as though it was pushing her towards the back of the garden.

'Maia! Hugo!'

Michelle turned the corner of the house and stood looking around the immaculate garden. The green grass was freshly shorn after Richmond's Saturday attentions. The pristine water of the infinity pool was still except for the rhythmic ripples that came from the pool cleaner as it made its journey along the bottom. She called Hugo's name again and thought she heard a slight rustle in the bushes and something that sounded like it could have been a whimper. She shaded her eyes and called but no Hugo came out. Michelle felt an eeriness hanging over the garden. She was about to return to the house when she saw something bobbing in the pool.

It was Maia's Barbie doll.

Michelle began to run.

She came to a stop at the edge of the pool and looked down.

Time stood still for what seemed like a second and then like an eternity. Michelle stared and stared. The pool cleaner was jammed against something at the bottom of the pool, sucking at it, making a gurgling, straining noise.

It was Maia.

Michelle's temporary paralysis was replaced by a rush of adrenalin and she dived into the pool, discarding her shoes with frantic kicks as she went deeper under the water. She grasped the little girl by the arm and pulled her towards her. Using all her strength, she pushed Maia towards the surface.

Michelle gasped and gulped for air as she surfaced. Desperately, she grabbed Maia's head and lifted it so that her face was out of the water. She kicked her legs, pushing Maia towards the steps in the shallow end. As soon as the water was shallow enough for her to stand she gathered the child in her arms. She laid her on the brick paving by the side of the pool.

Her mind in a whirl and panic setting in, Michelle started to shake Maia by her shoulders. Then she stuck her fingers in her mouth and turned her head to one side in an attempt to expel the water she must have swallowed. Maia didn't respond to anything she did. Michelle had done a first aid course five years ago but she found herself drawing a blank as she stared down at Maia's motionless body. She looked around desperately, trying to figure out what to do next, the shock of the moment overwhelming her.

Michelle screamed for help, but even as she screamed, she knew it was useless. She needed help and she needed it quickly. She ran inside the house and grabbed her cellphone from the kitchen counter, dialling the emergency services as she ran back outside. The call connected just as she reached the swimming pool and knelt down next to Maia. She began to shake her in another attempt to stir her but Maia lay mute, staring up into the sky.

'You're through to Netcare 911. In case of emergency ...'

'PICK UP!' Michelle screamed at the voice recording.

'... please press 1.'

Michelle pressed 1 and waited. 'Wake up, Maia,' she whispered urgently. '*Please* wake up.'

'Netcare 911, how may I assist you?'

'I need an ambulance at number 76 5th Avenue in Parkhurst,' Michelle said as clearly as possible, not wanting to lose a second on miscommunication. 'A little girl fell in the swimming pool ...'

'Okay, ma'am. I'm dispatching paramedics as we speak. While they make their way to you I need to ask you some questions that will help them when they arrive.'

'Okay, okay. Thank you.'

'How old is the child?'

'Five! She's five!'

'Is there anyone there who can perform CPR?'

'I did a course a while back but I can't remember any of it.'

'How long has the child been in the water?'

Michelle looked down at Maia and realised that she had absolutely no clue. The last 20 minutes or so had been a blur of phone calls.

'Excuse me, ma'am,' the operator said. 'Did you hear the question? How long has the child been in the water?'

'I don't know,' Michelle said, breaking down. 'I don't know.'

chapter 27

RACHEL SAT UP in bed as soon as she heard the car horn blare out from the storm, the desperation in the sound striking fear into her heart. She looked around and waited, trying to figure out if it was real or a figment of her imagination. Then she heard the same sound she had heard earlier, someone crying out, only this time she recognised it as a human sound. She heard it again, weaker maybe but no less desperate. She climbed out of bed and went over to the window. Pulling the curtain aside, she peered out into the rain.

She took an involuntary step backwards when a flash of lightning lit up the sky but she had seen something odd. She waited for the roll of thunder to finish and looked back out. It was Michelle. She was on her hands and knees, collapsed in the middle of the driveway beside her car, the rain beating down on her. Rachel stared at her, trying to understand what on earth had brought the woman outside in the middle of the storm. When Michelle cried out once more, this time clearly in pain, Rachel realised what was happening.

Instinctively, she moved towards the door but then stopped herself. She returned to the window. She put her face right up against the glass, like Maia used to do, and watched Michelle struggle. This was it, Rachel thought to herself. This was the justice she had been crying out for. After all that had been taken from her, here she was about to witness her vindication play out in front of her. A dark wave of warmth moved through her body. She stood very still and she watched.

She watched in silence as Michelle battled the elements, crawling closer to her car to find shelter. Her body looked as though it was responding to ripples of pain and she moaned in agony as she edged her way along the rough paving.

All of a sudden the sky was illuminated by a huge sheet of lightning. For a brief second Rachel saw her face reflected back at her in the glass. Then came the loudest crack yet, probably the loudest Rachel had ever heard. She jumped back in terror. There was a strange scorched smell in the air. As she tried to keep her balance, she knocked the biscuit tin off the table and it crashed down, spilling all of its contents across the floor. Rachel looked down, her heart still thumping with fright. There was a photograph face-down beside her foot. She picked it up.

It was Maia's school photograph. Staring down at her smiling child, the child she had lost, a band of pain seared through her as sharply as any lightning bolt, and simultaneously another weak cry came from the driveway. She leant against the wall and began to weep. With the flow of her tears something else seemed to be flowing through her, a multitude of emotions, the weight of which compelled her to the floor. Rachel sat heavily, the photograph held tight against her breast, and wept and wept.

As much as she wanted justice for what had been taken from her, she knew that she couldn't allow another woman, no matter how much she hated her, to feel what she had felt when Maia had been ripped from her life. It was a wound that could never be healed. She could not intentionally inflict that on someone else.

Pushing herself to her feet, Rachel went over to the door and walked out into the driving rain.

chapter 28

RACHEL'S VISIT TO Home Affairs had been as expected: uncomfortable and humiliating. The taxi journey home had taken longer than anticipated and she had arrived at the taxi rank at 13:45, which left her with fifteen minutes to get back to the Jordaans' house before she was late for Michelle. Adjusting her handbag, Rachel picked up the pace, her heels clicking loudly on the tar of the tree-lined street.

She felt a stone inside her shoe and stopped for a moment to get rid of it, balancing on one leg as she took her shoe off and knocked it against the side of her thigh. She was about to start walking again when she sensed that something wasn't right. Looking around the empty street, she tried to pinpoint what it was that was disturbing her – whether it was residue from her experience at Home Affairs or something else that she couldn't identify.

The feeling of unrest continued to grow and she started to walk faster, holding onto her bag and papers so that she didn't drop them. She was two blocks away from the house when she heard the sound of a horn behind her and turned to see Chris's car pulling up to the kerb.

'Why are you running?' Chris asked through his open window.

'I'm late,' Rachel replied, suddenly feeling foolish in front of Chris. 'Michelle said I must be back by two.'

'Well, jump in the car then,' Chris said as he cleared shopping bags from the front passenger seat for her. 'I'm heading home as well.'

There was no use in arguing so for the second time that day Rachel opened the door and lowered herself into the Z4. She put on her seatbelt and tried to ignore the strange feeling of dread that still sat heavily on her heart.

Chris was grinning at her. He looked very pleased with himself. He put the car into first gear and zoomed off.

'Why are you home so early today, Chris?' Rachel asked.

'You're not going to believe it,' Chris said, a huge smile on his face, 'but we just found out: Michelle is pregnant. We're having a baby!'

'That's great news,' Rachel said, smiling back at him. 'You will make a good father.'

Chris slowed as they came up to an amber traffic light and pulled to a stop. As he waited for the light to change to green, he turned to Rachel in the passenger seat. He was about to ask her something when the sound of an emergency siren filled the air and he glanced up in the rear view mirror. Rachel turned around to look too. An ambulance was hurtling up behind them, its red lights flashing and siren blaring. Chris quickly pulled the car to the side to make way for it to pass and they watched as it sped across the intersection and disappeared down the road.

'I hate that sound,' Chris said as the traffic light turned green and he moved the car forward, more slowly this time. 'Always makes me feel horrible.' He shuddered.

Rachel nodded and looked at the clock on the dash, the time reading 13:57. She had three minutes before she was officially late but now she knew that the Jordaans would be too distracted by the news of the baby to care about it, so she wasn't as tense.

They turned the corner, the one where she sat and socialised with Maria and Tapiwa, and drove into the Jordaans' street. The ambulance that had been in such a hurry was parked further down, its lights still flashing. Rachel leaned forward curiously to see whose property it was, realising at the same time as Chris did that it seemed to be theirs. The ambulance had stopped outside the Jordaans' house.

'What the – ?'

Chris pulled over behind the ambulance and yanked up the handbrake. He scrambled out of the car and Rachel followed his lead, bringing her bag and papers with her. She watched Chris approach the driver of the ambulance, a young man who looked fresh out of training.

'What's going on here?' she heard Chris ask.

'Sir, I'm going to need you to – '

'I live here.'

'Sir, we received an emergency call to this address and – '

Chris didn't wait for the driver to finish his sentence. He ran through the side gate into the property, calling out for Michelle as he went. Rachel stared at the open doors at the back of the ambulance. The vehicle was empty except for lots of what was obviously medical equipment. The flashing red lights on wet tar – there must have been a shower earlier – were harsh on her eyes. As she walked through the side gate she saw two paramedics with bags in their hands run past her room and down the path that led to the back garden.

Rachel's heart started pounding, the fear from earlier returning with a greater sense of urgency. Placing her bag and papers on the ground next to her room, she slowly started to walk down the pathway, then picked up speed as sudden fear clamped around her heart. As she rounded the corner she saw a group of people, she couldn't tell how many, at the side of the swimming pool. Some were kneeling, while a couple of others stood and handed gear back and forth. She saw Chris with his back to her.

The air was filled with a horrible shrieking sound that was but wasn't human and Rachel put her hands over her ears. She realised that she'd heard it from the road. The sound was coming from the pool itself and she stared across at the water to try and identify it. It was the pool cleaner, stuck against the side and partly above the surface. As it gasped at the air it made an eerie screeching noise that sounded like somebody crying in torment.

Rachel returned her attention to the paramedics, who were giving instructions to each other. She tried to see what they were doing, but she was reluctant to go any closer, not wanting to intrude.

As the wall of people shifted around, she caught a glimpse of something on the brick paving. Or someone. Someone was lying on the ground there by the side of the pool. The group shifted again, moving back a little, making her view momentarily clearer. She saw a hand. A child's hand.

Rachel's legs buckled but she didn't fall. She was aware of Chris's face turning towards her as she began to run.

Chris met her halfway there and he grabbed her and held her tightly, his strong frame preventing her from moving forward. Like a wild thing she clawed at him and screamed – 'Maia! Maia!' – lunging and twisting in his arms, almost knocking him over. But Chris stood firm and held onto her until she surrendered, until he was able to draw her face into his chest and hold her there until her screams quietened.

He loosened his grip slightly and Rachel was able to turn her head and look over at the group of people by the pool. Two of them had moved aside and were standing apart from the others, turning their heads to look over to where she and Chris were standing, talking in low voices. Now she could see Maia clearly. She was lying on her back in her princess dress. She heard snatches of what the paramedics bending over her daughter were saying to each other.

'No response ...' she thought she heard one of them say.

The other, a middle-aged white man in a white shirt, whom she recognised as one of the two men running past her room with their bags, was pushing down violently on Maia's chest. When the other paramedic put a hand on the man's shoulder and shook his head, he stood up.

Rachel let out one last scream and then all of her strength left her body. She felt herself falling. Chris supported her as she went down, bracing himself in case she tried to break away again and run.

Rachel tried to stand up but couldn't. From the grass she looked across helplessly to the pool and that was when she saw Michelle. She was standing behind the paramedics, Maia's body between her and them, her head bowed. Her clothes were soaking wet.

chapter 29

MICHELLE LOOKED UP as the door to Rachel's room opened and Rachel stepped out into the pouring rain, the cold wind slamming her in the face. She started to shake her head – no, no – and tried to get up but Rachel kept coming towards her. As she looked up at the woman whose life she had broken, tears began to run down her face.

'Not you!' Michelle cried. 'Anyone but you.' She turned her head away. 'Please don't help me,' she begged. 'Just leave me out here.'

Rachel ignored her. She knelt down next to Michelle and allowed her eyes a couple of seconds to get accustomed to the darkness before trying to assess the situation. Michelle struggled against her, using all the strength she could muster to push her away.

'Leave me alone!' she shouted, wincing in pain.

Rachel sat back on her heels and waited. When Michelle's fierce resistance gave way to gentle sobbing and she curled up on her side on the brickwork in the driveway and closed her eyes, Rachel leaned forward. She cleared some of the leaves and dirt from the flooded driveway that had caught in Michelle's matted hair.

'I need to get you inside,' she said. She began trying to lift Michelle.

'No,' Michelle pleaded. She curled tighter. 'I deserve this … Rachel, I …'

Rachel's expression was calm and so were her next words.

'Nobody does,' she said.

Michelle didn't know how to respond to this kindness, this forgiveness, but found she didn't have time to dwell on the moment as the next contraction slammed her back to reality. She let out a sharp cry.

Rachel manoeuvred her arm beneath Michelle's shoulders and got her to a half-sitting position. 'You have to move,' she said. 'Come. I will help you.'

'I can't,' Michelle panted. 'I … can't … move …'

Rachel lowered her back onto the driveway on her back and stood up, considering the options. She looked around. She could feel Michelle's panic-stricken eyes on her.

'I can feel the baby coming,' Michelle said.

'I'm going to fetch some blankets from my room,' Rachel said.

She ran back to her room and returned with the blue blanket from her bed and her two pillows. She also had a clean spare towel from her bathroom. She folded the blanket quickly and laid it on the ground. As she tried to roll Michelle onto it, so that it was around her pelvis, another flash of lightning streaked across the sky. Michelle saw Rachel flinch and duck down in fear but she was powerless to prevent a loud moan at that moment. The baby was definitely coming.

Rachel knelt down in front of Michelle, pulling her pants off so that she could see how far along the baby was.

'I need you to lie back against the pillows – they're right behind your head – and get ready to push,' Rachel said.

'I can't do this, not in the *driveway*,' Michelle cried out, some of her old fire returning.

'I need you to stay focused. The baby is almost here.'

'And *I* need to get to the hospital,' Michelle retorted.

'It's too late for the hospital,' Rachel said firmly. 'Trust me, you'll be fine.'

'How do you know?'

'I just do,' Rachel replied, her tone inviting no argument. 'I'm a nurse.'

Michelle looked up at her, confused. The information was new yet it was comforting. She let out another groan as she responded to the pain, exhaling in short, sharp breaths as she tried to activate the breathing technique she had been taught in the antenatal classes, which suddenly seemed completely inadequate.

'That's right,' Rachel encouraged her. 'We need to take this slowly. It's very important for you and the baby that we don't rush this. Don't push until I tell you to – even though you are going to want to.'

Michelle let out a cry and Rachel watched as she turned her face to the sky, closing her eyes, and allowing the rain to fall down on her. Even in the darkness she could see she was very pale, but she didn't need Michelle to see her anxiety.

'You won't have any anaesthetic or expensive equipment to help, but I promise you that your baby will be okay if you do what I say,' she said. 'Only push when I tell you to. Do you hear me?'

Michelle started to cry again, but she managed to nod her head.

Rachel rolled up her sleeves and leaned forward.

'Slowly now,' she said. She had her hands on Michelle's thighs.

Michelle shook her head and grabbed Rachel by the arm, trying to force her to look up into her desperate eyes.

'Rachel – '

'Focus on your child.' Rachel did not look at Michelle. 'Don't push yet.'

'I can't help it!'

'If you're talking, you're not going to be ready to push.'

Michelle grimaced in pain but tried to obey Rachel's instructions, even though the pain seemed to be growing with each second that passed and she felt like she was going to black out any minute.

Rachel could see that Michelle had taken in what she had said and was resisting the urge to push.

'The baby is ready,' she said. 'I want you to push on the next contraction.'

Michelle gritted her teeth and waited for the wave of pain before she pushed down. The baby's head slid through the birth canal into Rachel's ready hands.

'You're doing well,' Rachel said, supporting the delicate head. 'Take another breath and push again.'

Michelle obeyed, her effort resulting in the baby's shoulders appearing. One more groan pushed the new life into Rachel's hands and Michelle lay back, utterly exhausted. The rain continued to bucket down, washing away the blood and mucus that covered the baby's tiny body. Rachel held the baby up so that Michelle could see it, taking care not to pull too hard on the umbilical cord.

And then the night air was filled with a shrill cry, another one, the sound of new life calling out to let the world know that it existed, and Michelle and Rachel exhaled in simultaneous relief. Their eyes met briefly.

Michelle watched as a smile broke out across Rachel's wet face. Rahel reached for one of the towels that she had brought out with her. Michelle saw how tenderly she wrapped the baby in the towel, carefully avoiding the cord that was still attached to her.

'It's a girl,' Rachel said. 'You have a daughter.'

Rachel positioned the crying baby in Michelle's arms and sat back on her heels. Michelle tried to take this miracle in, and in the instant they touched each other, she knew without a shadow of doubt that an unshakable love had been created between her and her child.

Rachel placed a hand on her knee to get her attention.

'I'm going to go to the pay phone to call for an ambulance,' she said. 'You need to stay awake and hold onto her until I get back.'

Rachel used her house keys to open the side gate. Running through the rain, she made her way to the pay phone and dialled the emergency services. After giving them all the information they needed to know, she started walking back. She realised that she was exhausted, too, and suddenly extremely cold. The walking was slow going. There were almost no cars on the road at this time of night and in such a bad storm, but finally it seemed that the rain was easing up a little. In the silence, in the distance, she could hear the wail of a siren and a few minutes later an ambulance came speeding past her. She had left the side gate open for them and, as she turned the corner and approached the Jordaans' property, she saw the flashing red lights up ahead. She felt a tightening in her chest but she walked on at the same steady pace.

The paramedics were already attending to Michelle and the baby by the time she reached the driveway. She stood holding the gate open. Within minutes they had Michelle on a stretcher. As they wheeled her through Michelle looked up at Rachel, her eyes filled with relief and gratitude. Rachel acknowledged and returned the look. Only they knew what they had experienced together and no words right now, or ever probably, could adequately describe it.

Rachel waited for the ambulance to leave. Then she closed and locked the side gate and, using Michelle's keys, she entered the dark house and made her way through to the kitchen, almost tripping over Hugo, who was at her ankles, whining pitifully. Soothing the frightened dog with her voice, she went straight to the cupboard where the mains were and flipped through the switches, but the power was still out from the storm. She opened the cupboard beneath the sink and took out some plain white candles, two candle holders and a box of matches. She stuck the candles in the holders and lit them, cupping the flames with her hands as she carried them one by one over to the big wooden table. They suffused the room with a beautiful soft light.

Looking around the kitchen, Rachel saw that Hugo was back in his basket, his nose tucked between his paws. She refilled his water bowl and made sure that there were pellets in his food bowl. Then she walked over to the sink and turned on the tap, testing the flow with her fingers to make sure there was still some hot water. As she let it run over the dirty dishes, she reached under the basin for the dishwashing liquid.

When she was done with the dishes Rachel moved on to the rest of the house, taking the candles with her into each room, restoring order to the place in the way she knew best. She knew that her time with the Jordaans was over, that there were some things that just couldn't be undone. She and Michelle would never share a meal or live together again and there was no use pretending that they might. But she would leave them with dignity. She could do that now.

Chris ran down the corridor of the Sandton Mediclinic, following the directions the receptionist had given him. It had been just after three in the morning when he'd received the call from the hospital and somehow he had managed to secure a seat on a flight to Johannesburg that left King Shaka Airport at 06:30.

Dr Pieterse was waiting for him in the reception area. She told him she didn't know the full story, but it seemed that Michelle had gone into labour prematurely in the middle of the previous night's electrical storm, which had blown the power and left her unable to telephone for assistance herself. Someone who lived on the property – a nurse, was it? Michelle had been exhausted and apparently slightly delirious too – had safely delivered the baby. They were both absolutely fine, she reassured Chris, but she wanted to keep them in for a few nights just to be sure. The baby was a couple of weeks premature and might also have a touch of jaundice so they were treating it in the neonatal high care unit.

All the drama aside, she said, Chris and Michelle were the proud parents of a baby girl.

A girl!

Despite his anxiety, as he ran down the corridor Chris couldn't hide his smile.

He slowed to a fast walk, checking the numbers on the rooms until he reached room 215. He stopped to catch his breath, then quietly opened the door. The curtains around Michelle's bed were drawn and he peeped inside. Michelle was asleep. Dr Pieterse had suggested he not wake her if she was. He stood with his arms at his sides watching her lying there, and in that moment he felt an overwhelming surge of love for his wife. He realised he couldn't bear the thought of her being in any kind of pain or distress. The animosity and tension that had separated them for the last few months didn't seem important any more. Mostly what Chris felt at that precise moment was profoundly grateful that he would have a chance to love Michelle and keep loving her.

He heard footsteps behind him and turned. It was a nurse. She smiled at him and put her hand on his shoulder.

'Dr Pieterse asked me to take you to the neonatal unit,' she said. 'Are you ready to see your baby?'

The rhythmic hum of machines and other complicated-looking equipment that powered the incubators was what Chris noticed first. Nurses moved around quietly and several of the babies in the incubators had one or two people standing or sitting beside them. At the far end of the sterile room was an incubator which looked unattended.

The nurse led him towards it and then she stood back and allowed Chris to approach the glass-covered incubator on his own. Inside a tiny baby lay on its back – his daughter. Her little head was covered with a dusting of fine, blonde hair and her eyes were tightly closed. Chris watched the small chest rise and fall, her breathing fast and shallow, and tried to take all of her in. His eyes moist with emotion, he looked around to see if any of the other parents were as enamoured with their newborns as he was.

It would seem that they were.

He returned his attention to his daughter. The pink hospital band tied around her small foot hung loosely and he peered at the writing on it: 'Jordaan'.

Something like relief, only a much bigger emotion he had no name for, filled his heart. It was as if for months he and Michelle had been held captive, with a yoke around their necks, but now, suddenly, in some imperfect way the yoke had been broken.

Having been assured by the nurse that Michelle would be unlikely to wake until the afternoon, Chris went home to let Hugo out and to make sure that their house was still in one piece after the previous night's storm.

Michelle's Audi was halfway up the driveway. He looked through the window at the ignition but the keys weren't in it and the car was locked. Walking through the front door, he was surprised to find that everything was in perfect order. In the kitchen the dishes were stacked in the drying rack. Michelle's car keys were on the wooden table beside a blob of melted white wax. He looked at the clock on the wall in the kitchen; it was a little after nine. Clean, washed clothes, freshly ironed, were in two neat piles on the counter. Hugo greeted him with great enthusiasm, furiously wagging his tail and giving little barks of delight. There was food in his bowl, and a full bowl of clean water.

Rachel. Of course.

Chris went back to the front door and opened it. He began to walk up to Rachel's room, trying to put together and process what must have happened the previous evening. Could Rachel have been the 'nurse'?

He knocked and, when there was no response, tried the handle. The door was open. He went inside and he saw that the room was empty. All of Rachel's personal items were gone. On the table in the middle of the room, next to her set of keys, was a plain white envelope. He walked over and picked it up. It wasn't sealed. He pulled out a folded piece of paper. He recognised it at once and knew at the same time that they would never see Rachel again and that this dark chapter in all of their lives was closed.

It was a drawing that Maia had done.

A stick figure mother and a stick figure child in a green and blue princess dress were strolling along a beach together hand in hand. There was a stripe of blue sea behind them and a bright yellow sun in the corner of the page shining down.

epilogue

RACHEL CLIMBED OUT of the taxi, the warm Mozambican wind greeting her with the fragrance of saltwater and jasmine. The driver placed her two suitcases at the side of the dirt road. She counted out the remainder of the fare and thanked him.

She had managed to get R8 000 for Michelle's earrings and, after spending R1 000 on the journey back home, she reckoned she still had enough left over to last her family for a couple of months before she would be forced to look for work again. She felt no guilt over the theft, nor did she feel as though it was owed to her because of what she had done for Michelle.

It was what it was.

Waiting around for the Jordaans to return from the hospital had not been an option and she had left them with no way of contacting her. She did not need to see the baby nor endure Chris and Michelle's futile attempts to try and fix the situation with guilt money or the offer of keeping her job. As far as she was concerned that portion of her life lay at the bottom of an infinity pool in Johannesburg and would forever stay there.

She hadn't said goodbye to Tapiwa, believing that the more cleanly she cut the ties with her life in the city the better. Besides, Tapiwa and Maria were both women who understood how their world worked and they would not hold her decision against her; each would have done the same in her position.

Rachel held tightly onto the urn that contained Maia's ashes and stood gazing around at the streets of her childhood, the market milling with people and the stall holders beginning to close up their stands for the day. She could hear the ocean and she felt its pull. She was tempted to leave her bags just where they were and run towards it, to feel her feet dig into the soft white sand again, her toes feeling for the cool water beneath.

The next few days were not going to be easy but she thought she knew how to handle them. She would tell her parents how Maia had died but would leave out Michelle's involvement and the date that it had happened. It was better if they believed it was a recent event. They would mourn together and have a church service, scatter her ashes and mourn some more. Rachel would lay Maia to rest over the aquamarine waters of the Bazaruto Archipelago and in so doing she felt that, in some way at least, she would be honouring and fulfilling her daughter's wish to swim in the ocean.

And, when the sound of weeping had left their home, Rachel would look for work once again, first in Inhassoro, then Maputo and, if life demanded it, in South Africa again. She would take whatever work she could get so that she could support her parents and, when their time came to move on, she would figure out what her next step would be. For now all that mattered was that she was home and that Maia was with her.

a note from the author

My stories are always sparked by a simple image or idea and *Rachel Weeping* was no different. The idea for the book was birthed in 2002 when I stumbled upon a Hebrew text that was written by the prophet Jeremiah around 600 BC and was echoed later in early Christian writings by the apostle Matthew. It reads:

jeremiah 31:15
'A voice is heard in Ramah,
lamentation, weeping, great mourning,
Rachel weeping for her children and
refusing to be comforted,
because they are no more.'

This passage conjured up the image of a woman holding tightly to the body of a young child, mourning the loss of her beloved, and became the foundation for the story that you are now holding. As the years flew by, layers and textures were added to it and, as the story grew, so did the desire to explore the experience of the foreign nationals from neighbouring countries who are trying to earn a living in my home country, South Africa.

South Africa's legacy is apartheid and, in many ways, in this environment it was much easier to determine right from wrong.

It was a defined legal system that was rooted in inequality and was one that the objective mind could easily point at and say, with certainty, 'This is wrong.'

Apartheid was abolished in 1994 and what we now face is a blurry system of economic, political and educational injustice that is not as easy to identify and change. It is not a set of laws but rather a culture that exists in the uneasy tension between those who have and those who don't, those who are legal citizens and those who are not.

But this is not a tension that is unique to South Africa. *Rachel Weeping* could just as easily have played out in Los Angeles with a Mexican domestic worker or in London with an Eastern European. Rachel could have been a Filipino working in Sydney or a Pakistani in Dubai and it is this reality that makes this story and its themes a universal one.

My goal in all of this was not to take the obvious choice and demonise the Jordaans, telling yet another story about the poor immigrant suffering at the hand of the wealthy employer. That would simplify a situation that just isn't simple and would play to stereotypes rather than explore both sides of the story. At the end of the day, this narrative is purely a mirror that I have held up to myself and hopefully the reader so that, in some small way, we can all hear the voice of 'the other' in our lives, whoever that other may be.

It was only once I had finished writing this novel that I went back to the passages that had birthed it and saw that the original Hebrew text had been written for an audience that was in exile, a people forced by circumstances to live in a land that was not their own.

And, as I read beyond the passage that inspired this story of loss, I was pleasantly surprised to read the words that followed the prophet's description of mourning. He goes on to write:

jeremiah 31:16-17
'Restrain your voice from weeping
and your eyes from tears,
for your work will be rewarded,'
declares the LORD.
'They will return from the land of the enemy.
So there is hope for your descendants,'
declares the LORD.
'Your children will return to their own land.'

In many ways this passage is my wish for Rachel and for the Rachels who live amongst us, a promise of hope and of restoration. Alas, I have seen too much of this world to believe that everyone's story ends well and believe that it would be naive to think that this promise will be fulfilled for all who are mourning in my lifetime.

But I do have hope.

Brett Michael Innes
Johannesburg, South Africa

PS Thank you to all who have helped bring this story to life. It takes a village ...

READING GROUP QUESTIONS

1. If you employ a domestic worker or gardener, describe your relationship with them.
2. If you are employed in a minimum wage job, describe your relationship with the people you serve.
3. Is it the responsibility of an employer to look after their staff and their family in the way that the Jordaans looked after Rachel and Maia?
4. What is the difference between minimum wage and a 'living wage'?
5. Should you employ people who are in your country illegally, even if they are cheaper than legal labour?
6. Is it your nation's responsibility to look after citizens of another nation, especially if they don't pay tax?
7. Rachel steals from Michelle but uses the money to support her family – what do you think of this?
8. Do you think Rachel was justified in hiding her occupation from the other mothers at Maia's school?
9. What do you think of Rachel and Michelle's relationship before the drowning? Do you think there was a genuine friendship?
10. Brett, the author, is a white South African male with a private school education who has travelled extensively into Africa working with NGOs. To what extent do you feel this influenced the writing of *Rachel Weeping* and his portrayal of both the Jordaans and Rachel?
11. What do you think of the novel's ending?
12. What imagery stood out for you and why?

a note about the author

Born in 1983 in Johannesburg, South Africa, Brett Michael Innes spent three years working as a documentary photographer and filmmaker with various NGOs, a position that has seen him and his camera travel into war zones and malnutrition clinics across the continent. His first novel, *The Story of Racheltjie de Beer*, was released in 2012 and became a South African bestseller, hitting top positions on both local and international charts.

Brett works closely with Joint Aid Management, a South African based NGO that focuses on bringing food and water relief to South Sudan, Angola, Mozambique and South Africa, and has participated in many of their trips into these regions. Visit Joint Aid Management on www.jamint.com to find out more about their programmes.

GET SOCIAL WITH BRETT

Author Website	www.brettmichaelinnes.com
Facebook	www.facebook.com/BrettMichaelInnes
Twitter	www.twitter.com/BrettMInnes
Instagram	www.instagram.com/brettmichaelinnes